Evidence Beyond a Reasonable Doubt

You Will Never Die

R. Craig Hogan, PhD

Copyright © 2021 by Greater Reality Publications

You may make copies of the text for any purpose that helps you or humankind develop spiritually. Don't charge money for anything in the book. Give it away freely. Please put the name of the book, copyright Greater Reality Publications, and the website (http://earthschoolanswers.com) on the first page of any copies you make.

GR

Greater Reality Publications
23 Payne Place, Normal, IL 61761
http://greaterreality.com
800 690-4232
Email: info@greaterreality.com

ISBN Paperback: 978-1-7374106-8-3
ISBN ePub: 978-1-7374106-9-0

Other Books by Dr. R. Craig Hogan

Your Eternal Self: Science Discovers the Afterlife

There Is Nothing but Mind and Experiences

*Reasons for What Happens to You
in Your Life & Your Afterlife*

*Answers to Life's Enduring Questions
from Science Discoveries and Afterlife Revelations*

*Induced Afterlife Communication:
A Miraculous Therapy for Grief and Loss*

*Repair & Reattachment Grief Therapy:
Guided Afterlife Connections*

*Afterlife Communication:
16 Proven Methods, 85 True Accounts*

New Developments in Afterlife Communication

*Aspects of Consciousness:
Proceedings of the 40th Annual ASCS Conference*

Afterlife Resources from AREI

The books are all available on Amazon.

Contents

Preface vii

Content of This Book x

First Area of Evidence You Will Never Die: Communication with People Whose Bodies Have Died..1

Chapter 1: Direct-Voice or Independent-Voice Communication Is Evidence You Will Never Die..5

1. Dr. Dinshaw Nanji Communicates with His Wife, Annie, Living in the Next Life..5
2. Alice Fearon Communicates with Her Son in Spirit 17
3. Eira Conacher Communicates with Her Husband, Douglas, Living in the Life after This Life 20
4. David Cattanach Communicates with His Mother in Sessions with Leslie Flint 23

Evidence from Direct-Voice Mediumship Proves You Will Never Die 25

Chapter 2: Communication through Materialization Mediumship Is Evidence You Will Never Die..26

1. A Man Whose Body Is Dead Speaks to His Love 26
2. Konstantin Raudive Materializes and Speaks to Sonia Rinaldi 32
3. Carlos Mirabelli Produces Two Materializations of Individuals before Witnesses 36
4. Helen Duncan's Trial Witnesses Confirm the Materializations of People They Know Intimately 39
5. Montague Keen Materializes and Speaks to People Who Knew Him in This Life 55

Evidence from Materialization Mediumship Proves You Will Never Die 58

Contents

Chapter 3: Communication through Instrumental Transcommunication Is Evidence You Will Never Die 61

1. Sonia Rinaldi's Instrumental Transcommunication 62
2. Sheri Perl's Instrumental Transcommunication 65
3. Konstantin Raudive's Recorded Phone Calls from the Life after This Life to Well-Known Individuals 69
4. George Meek and Bill O'Neil's Recorded Conversations with a Scientist in the Next Life 70

Evidence from Instrumental Transcommunication Proves You Will Never Die 71

Chapter 4: Appearances by People after Their Bodily Deaths Are Evidence You Will Never Die 73

1. Elisabeth Kübler-Ross Experiences a Materialization 73
2. Raymond A. Moody Experiences and Speaks with His Deceased Grandmother 76
3. Rev. John Bertram Phillips Experiences a Materialization of C. S. Lewis 77
4. People Appear to Loved Ones a Distance Away at the Moment of Their Transition 79

Evidence from Appearances by People Whose Bodies Have Died Proves You Will Never Die 82

Chapter 5: Psychotherapist Afterlife Communication Experiences Are Evidence You Will Never Die 83

1. Induced After-Death Communication Demonstrates That Consciousness Survives Bodily Death 83
2. Repair & Reattachment Grief Therapy Helps People Have Afterlife Communication 88
3. Loving Heart Connections Have Been Shown to Help People Communicate with Loved Ones 90

Evidence from Psychotherapist Connections Proves You Will Never Die 93

Chapter 6: Self-Guided Afterlife Connections Are Evidence You Will Never Die 95

Evidence from Self-Guided Connections Proves You Will Never Die 98

Contents

Chapter 7: Communication through Trance Mediumship Is Evidence You Will Never Die 99

    1. Rev. Charles Drayton Thomas Communicates with His Father through Medium Gladys Osborne Leonard 100

    2. George Pelham Communicates with Richard Hodgson through Medium Leonora Piper 102

    3. Richard Hodgson Communicates with a Good Friend after His Friend's Bodily Death 104

    4. Family Members Verified Communication with Their Daughter Whose Body Had Died 105

    5. Flight Lieutenant H. C. Irwin Communicates to the British Air Ministry through Medium Eileen Garrett 106

    6. Raymond Lodge Communicates through Two Trance Mediums 108

    Evidence from Trance Mediumship Proves You Will Never Die 112

Chapter 8: Communication through Automatic Writing Is Evidence You Will Never Die 113

    Cross Correspondence 114

    1. The Mary Catherine Lyttelton Case 114

    2. The Myers Cross Correspondence Case 115

    Evidence of Communication through Automatic Writing Proves You Will Never Die 117

Chapter 9: Communication through Mental Mediumship Is Evidence You Will Never Die 119

    1. Canyon Ranch Experiment 119

    2. Study for an HBO Documentary 120

    3. The Miraval Silent-Sitter Experiment 120

    4. More Stringent Studies at the University of Arizona 121

    Evidence from Mental Mediumship Communication Proves You Will Never Die 121

Chapter 10: Communication Experiences in Dreams Are Evidence You Will Never Die 123

    1. Edgar Cayce and Dream Visitations 123

Contents

    2. Dream Visitations When the Dreamer Learns Things He or She Could Not Have Known 124

    3. The Nature of Dreams and the Afterlife Communication Experience 126

    Evidence from Dream Communications Proves You Will Never Die 127

Chapter 11: People's Common Afterlife Communication Experiences Are evidence You Will Never Die 129

    1. Studies of the Prevalence of Afterlife Communications Show They Are Common 129

    2. People Communicating with Those in the Next Life Learn Things They Couldn't Know Otherwise 131

    3. Pre-death and Deathbed Visions of Loved Ones Living in the Life after This Life Are Common 131

    Evidence from Common Afterlife Communication Proves You Will Never Die 135

Second Area of Evidence: The Nature of Reality and Consciousness Described by Science 137

Chapter 12: Evidence You Are a Manifestation of Our Universal Intelligence that Will Never Die 139

    1. Quantum Mechanics 140

    2. Experiences as the Content of Reality 142

    3. Near-Death Experiences of Blind People 143

    Evidence That You Are Our Universal Intelligence That Will Never Die 144

Chapter 13: Evidence Your Mind Is Not in Your Brain Means You Will Never Die 146

    1. Researchers Cannot Find a Mind in the Brain and Cannot Explain How a Brain Creates a Mind 146

    2. Researchers and Scientists Have Begun to Suggest the Mind Is Not in the Brain 147

    3. The Brain Doesn't Have the Capacity to Hold a Lifetime of Memories 149

    4. Psychics Know Information Not Available to Their Brains 149

    5. The Mind Knows Information before the Brain Has Access to It 151

    6. Consciousness Functions without Brain Involvement 153

Contents

7. People Commonly Describe Separating the Mind from the Body in Out-of-Body Experiences 158

8. Biophysicists Can Detect No Electrical Activity in Sensory Neurons That Have Been Assumed to Carry Sensory Information 160

Evidence Demonstrating That Your Mind Is Not in Your Brain Proves You Will Never Die 161

Chapter 14: Evidence from Near-Death Experiences Demonstrates You Will Live After Your Body Dies 162

1. More Acute Senses When They Should Be Failing 163

2. Knowledge about Distant People and Events When Bodies and Brains Have No Access 167

3. Knowledge That Is Not Understood but Later Validated 169

4. Feelings of Peace and Love Rather than Fear and Trauma 170

Evidence from Near-Death Experiences Proves You Will Never Die 171

Chapter 15: Highly Regarded Professionals Studying the Survival of Consciousness Have Concluded You Will Never Die 173

1. Physicians Acknowledge Life after This Life 173

2. Physical Scientists Who Have Studied Mediums Conclude Afterlife Communication Is Valid 174

3. Psychologists and Psychotherapists Have Concluded Afterlife Communication Is Valid 179

4. Professors of the Humanities Studying Afterlife Communication Have Concluded It Is Valid 183

5. Attorneys Who Have Studied Afterlife Communication 185

6. Clergy Who Have Studied Afterlife Communication Have Concluded It Is Possible and Valid 187

7. Church Bodies Who Have Studied Mediums Have Concluded the Communications Are Valid 188

8. Debunkers Who Have Studied Afterlife Communication Openly Conclude It Is Valid 189

Conclusion 191

The Message for Humankind 192

Contents

Endnotes 195

Bibliography 209

Preface

You are a spiritual being who will never die. You are having a brief experience in Earth School to learn lessons, grow in love and compassion, and enjoy life. When you graduate, you will go on to new, exciting experiences, but you will never see endings again as you see them on earth now. People you love will be with you on your new adventures. You will never die.

Your loved ones who have graduated before you are enjoying their new lives in peace and joy. You are not separated from them during this brief time when you and they are focusing your attention on different realms. They come to visit you often when they want to be part of what you are doing or when you ask them to come to you to talk or help you. Your loved ones are always only a thought away.

This book contains the evidence that you will live on after your body dies!

It will give you a new perspective. The archaic concepts that the universe is made of matter and energy independent of us, that our minds are in our brains, and that when the brain dies we die are primitive, naïve misconceptions. In this book you will learn that your mind will never cease to exist and that the Universal Intelligence our minds are part of together is continually creating what we experience as matter and energy, including our bodies and brains.

At one time, all people believed without doubt that the earth is the center of the universe. It seemed obvious to anyone who gazed at the starry canopy drifting across the sky at night and witnessed the sun rising in the east and setting in the west every day. The learned scientists of the day assured people that the earth is the center of the universe, ignoring Copernicus and Galileo when they proved the earth is simply a planet in a solar system with a sun at its center. Galileo was forced to recant his heretical views. In 1600 Giordano Bruno was burned alive for impudently asserting that stars were suns with planets around them.

Today all people know with confidence that the earth revolves around a sun that is itself revolving in the Milky Way galaxy, that is itself hurtling through a universe, that is itself expanding at 1.8 times the speed of light. Today everyone knows those facts. We feel they are self-evident, without a doubt. But it took hundreds of years of glacially slow mind changes for all people to believe them.

You and I are experiencing a similar revolution in thought today. Most people still aren't confident they will be alive after their bodies die and don't know what has happened to their loved ones whose bodies have died. They sob at funerals as though people have been deleted from all existence and will never be seen again. They solemnly walk across cemetery lawns to gaze at the ground where they believe their fathers, mothers, sons, and daughters are. Their children go with them, learning from their parents that when the body dies, it's a horror to be feared, and that they themselves will one day be buried in the ground or encased in a mausoleum. It's a terrible belief system that has no basis in truth, yet it holds humanity in its icy grip.

In another century or two after humankind has evolved to realize the truth about who we are, everyone will be certain, without question, that

- When the body dies, our minds, which were never integrated with the body, have just graduated from one school into the next school, which is filled with more love, peace, and joy than we can imagine.

- Those who have graduated before us are waiting for us there, alive, happy, and available to communicate with us if we just learn to listen.
- We are all of the same spiritual essence, of one substance in the body of Our Universal Intelligence.

The Garden of Eden is here, now. We are living in it. We were never driven from it. We drove ourselves into the illusion that we live in an unfeeling world of senseless matter and energy in which we are helpless victims unable to find happiness because the world is saturated with misery. We can dispel the illusion and waken in the Garden of Eden that has always been here. We can then reside in a world of love, peace, and happiness for the rest of our lives. All we must do is realize that what we are taught about life and reality are misconceptions perpetuated by a society that is intellectually in the Technological Age but spiritually in the Stone Age. The truth will be evident. Nothing else is required. It's all in our mind.

When you examine the evidence in this book, you will know with certainty that there is only Our Universal Intelligence at the basis of reality, that you are a living part of Our Universal Intelligence so you don't die when the body dies, that we are all one with each other, that you have unique purposes for being in Earth School, and that you will graduate to go on to a glorious life in the life after this life with all your loved ones.

The truth will set you free.

Content of This Book

The evidence in this book proves beyond a reasonable doubt that you will continue to live after your body dies. It confirms that our loved ones, whose bodies have died, are alive, well, and happy in the wonderful realm we too will enter. This evidence is organized into two areas:

First Area of Evidence You Will Never Die

> Verified communication with people whose bodies have been dead for years or decades demonstrates that consciousness survives bodily death.

Second Area of Evidence You Will Never Die

> The nature of reality and consciousness described by science demonstrates that
>
> - The universe is made of consciousness, and since you are a manifestation of that consciousness, you will never die.
>
> - Your mind is not in your brain so you will continue to live after your body and brain die.
>
> - As near-death experiences show, when your body and brain die, instead of becoming comatose you become more alert and joyous because you are entering the next realm of your eternal life.
>
> - Researchers, scientists, and other highly regarded professionals who have studied the life after this life and mediumship have concluded we do not die.

First Area of Evidence You Will Never Die

Communication with People Whose Bodies Have Died

We have many examples of individuals whose bodies have died communicating with people on earth who know them, proving beyond a reasonable doubt that we continue to live after our bodies die.

All of us live on after our bodies and brains die. So we should expect to have audio, photographic, video, and witness records of such communication. We should expect such encounters to be experienced by people on earth who can attest to the fact that the person they knew well in body is communicating. In fact, we have such records. We have recordings of individuals whose bodies died years or decades ago communicating with people who know them on earth. The recordings have the following characteristics that show these individuals are currently very much alive, even though their bodies have died:

- The individual whose body has died demonstrates fully functioning senses, mental capabilities, recognizable personality, fluent speech, memories of past experiences on earth, and recall from one session to the next of events with the person on this side of life. Their communication shows no degradation of any mental capacity that might conceivably occur when the body and brain die. The person communicating from this side of life knows the individual in spirit and can attest without a doubt that the personality communicating is that individual.

- The individual in spirit is aware of current occurrences in the lives of people alive on the earth plane. By entering the earth environment and observing events without being seen or otherwise detected, the individual in spirit correctly reports events that are corroborated by the person on this side of life.

- The individual in spirit knows the current thoughts and sentiments of the person on earth, who corroborates them. This demonstrates that the individual in spirit can communicate mind to mind, which is natural for residents of the life after this life, and that they continue to be in contact with people on this side of life through thoughts and sentiments.

- When the individual in spirit materializes, the materialized body has all the features and defects the individual had while living on the earth plane, demonstrating that it is they who are alive after their body has died.

Evidence exists in clear audio, video, photographic, and eyewitness accounts of sometimes lengthy communications between individuals in spirit and people on this side of life who can verify that the individuals are undeniably the people they knew.

The evidence in the next eleven chapters of this book shows that people whose bodies have died are still alive, proving beyond a reasonable doubt that you and those you love will never die—you will just go on to the next stage of your life. This evidence comprises the following:

- Direct-voice or independent-voice mediumship
- Materialization mediumship
- Instrumental transcommunication (electronic devices)
- Spontaneous materialization
- Psychotherapist-guided communication
- Self-guided afterlife communication
- Trance mediumship
- Automatic and planchette writing
- Mental mediumship
- Dreams
- Common afterlife communication experiences

Chapter 1

Direct-Voice or Independent-Voice Communication Is Evidence You Will Never Die

In direct-voice or independent-voice mediumship audio recordings, individuals alive in the life after this life communicate orally with people still on earth. Those on earth accept such conversations as valid because they recognize the individual in spirit's unique voice quality and personality as well as references to current events and reminiscences of past events in the people's lives.

1. Dr. Dinshaw Nanji Communicates with His Wife, Annie, Living in the Next Life

Summary

The Nanji recordings are evidence of the survival of consciousness. Chemistry professor Dr. Dinshaw Nanji communicated regularly with his wife, Annie Nanji, in spirit, through the mediumship of Leslie Flint. She spent much time unseen but close to Dr. Nanji as he went about his normal life activities, resulting in audio recordings of her comments about current events in Dr. Nanji's life.

Leslie Flint

The medium whose talents made the recordings possible was Leslie Flint, who lived from 1911 to 1994 in England. Flint would sit in a darkened room and a vocal mechanism would form on his shoulder from a substance produced by his body called ectoplasm. People living in the next life impressed their thoughts on the vocal mechanism so the thoughts were converted into audible voices using spirit energy. The vocal quality produced was the same as an announcer speaking into a microphone. Today we have thousands of recordings of voices communicating to loved ones sitting in the room with Flint.

The people on earth all expressed certainty that the voices belonged to their loved ones and that they were conversing with real, living persons, although their bodies had been dead, at times for decades.

Flint was tested mercilessly by a great number of scientists, magicians, and others determined to find fraud in what he did. The investigators put a throat microphone on him so any utterance would be recorded. They put colored water into his mouth, which was then sealed with Elastoplast tape. He returned the same-colored water to a glass after the séance. Throughout the large number of tests they never found a hint of fraud. Even when he sat in hotel rooms away from his accustomed surroundings, voices came through clearly.

The most conclusive evidence, however, that individuals whose bodies had died were speaking through the voice mechanism was that people in this life would come repeatedly, sometimes for years, to hold long, highly personal conversations with their loved ones in spirit. None of the participants on this side of life had any doubt they were speaking fluidly with the person they knew when that person was using a body. As you listen to the recordings that follow, you will hear a great variety of voices, male and female. It would be impossible for anyone to produce so many voices recognized by their loved ones, which demonstrates that the recordings contain the voices of people living in the life after this life.

Evidence for the validity of the Leslie Flint recordings can be found at www.afterlifeinstitute.org/validity/.

The recordings in this essay are from the archives of the Leslie Flint Educational Trust.[1]

Dr. Dinshaw Rattonji Nanji

In the following Leslie Flint session recordings, Dr. Dinshaw Rattonji Nanji, a professor in the Department of Biochemistry of Fermentation at the University of Birmingham in the U.K., speaks to his wife living in the life after this life. Dr. Nanji's identity as a capable, intelligent professional is verified. He published a number of papers on fermentation in journals such as the *Biochemistry Journal, Biochemical Journal, Journal of the Chemical Society*, and *Journal of the Society of the Chemical Industry*. He also holds U.S. patents for several processes, including treatment of plant materials in the preparation of fibers and a process for manufacturing textile yarns. The articles and patents are available today. Dr. Nanji retired from the university and moved from England to Gothenburg, Sweden.

Annie Ottilia Nanji

The body of Dr. Nanji's wife, Annie Ottilia Nanji, died of cancer in 1966. Between 1970 and 1983, Dr. Nanji traveled to London from Sweden repeatedly to communicate with his wife in sessions with Leslie Flint. Today, twenty recordings of the communications exist.

Evidence Proving That People Do Not Die When Their Bodies Die

Dr. Nanji's repeated trips to London and his conversations about intimacies only he and his wife would know demonstrate that Annie was alive, even though her body died in 1966. The recordings of Dr. Nanji's conversations with Annie demonstrate that Annie had full control of her senses, that her memory was intact, and that she had the same personality and mental faculties.

Following are the accounts of ten instances in which Annie refers to events in Dr. Nanji's life, which he corroborates. Links to the recordings on the Afterlife Research and Education Institute's website follow each description.

Communication 1 ~ Dr. Nanji has come to the session with Flint bringing Annie's wedding ring and a lock of her hair. Annie knows he has them and asks him about them. Listen at www.afterlifeinstitute.org/ring/.

Transcript of the recording:

Annie: You have got my ring in your pocket.

Dr. Nanji: Yes.

Annie: And also this lock of hair.

Dr. Nanji: Yes. Everything stays with me.

Annie: All the various things...

Dr. Nanji: Yes, Darling.

Annie: associated with us two.

Communication 2 ~ Annie has seen Dr. Nanji place a gravestone on her grave and that it has her name and his, but his has no date for his passing. She remarks about it. Listen at www.afterlifeinstitute.org/gravestone/.

Transcript of the recording:

Annie: And you know the gravestone where you have put your name but you are not there yet.

Dr. Nanji: No, but...

Annie: But you are very funny I have to laugh at you. You have on the gravestone you have got my name and date and now you have your name but no date. But you don't know when you are coming. But you will be able to have the date put in when you are here. They will make arrangements for you. There is room for you. But you won't be there, you will be with me. But it seems so strange that you should already arrange to put your name on the stone when you are not there yet.

Communication 3 ~ Annie has observed that Dr. Nanji has not changed anything in the flat since she transitioned. However, she has seen something that's not right. One of the bedspreads is not oriented correctly. Listen at www.afterlifeinstitute.org/bedspread/.

Transcript of the recording:

Annie: And you haven't changed anything. Everything in the flat is identically the same as when I left it.

Dr. Nanji: Exactly.

Annie: But there is a difference though, the bed covers.

Dr. Nanji: The bed covers, yes.

Annie: There is something different about the bed covers.

Dr. Nanji:	You bought those bed covers, Darling, the yellow ones.
Annie:	Yes, but have you done something to one of the bed covers?
Dr. Nanji:	No, Darling, they are identical.
Annie:	Well perhaps it is that they are the same bed covers but there is something different. I don't know what. Perhaps it is the way I see it.
Dr. Nanji:	But they are very nice and because you bought them, I like them very much.
Annie:	Are you sure you have them the right way around?
Dr. Nanji:	I bet not.
Annie:	I think that is why. Because I think you've got one of the … when you have the bed cover it is not always the right way around.
Dr. Nanji:	That may be, yes.
Annie:	I am certain that is so. Because it doesn't look right.

In the next session Annie has with Leslie Flint, she tells Dr. Nanji that he has adjusted the bedspread. He agrees.

Transcript for an excerpt of the recording:

Annie:	I see you have made a difference with the spread of the … bedspread.
Dr. Nanji:	Aha, yes, Darling.

Communication 4 ~ Dr. Nanji remarks that he hears Annie tapping in his flat to get his attention. She responds by saying she appreciates his consistent response: "Thank you, Darling." Listen at www.afterlifeinstitute.org/tapping/.

Transcript of the recording:

Dr. Nanji: Because, you know, I hear your tapping.

Annie: Good.

Dr. Nanji: And I am surprised at myself that I can hear it.

Annie: I always know when you hear, because you always acknowledge it.

Dr. Nanji: Yes, exactly.

Annie: And you always say, "Thank you, Darling."

Dr. Nanji: [Laughing] Yes, I know.

Communication 5 ~ Dr. Nanji has pictures Annie would like him to put up over the bed in his flat. Listen at www.afterlifeinstitute.org/pictures/.

Transcript of an excerpt of the recording:

Annie: Ah, everything is very much the same. You have not altered anything.

Dr. Nanji: No dar–

Annie: And you're going to put the pictures over the bed.

Dr. Nanji: Yes.

Annie: Just as we would wish, ah.

In the next session, Annie says she has seen the pictures he has put up in the flat and is delighted. She says she puts light around them that Dr. Nanji notices.

Annie: I am so thrilled with the pictures. You have got them in a very good prominent location. And you know sometimes you see the light around them?

Dr. Nanji: Yes.

Annie: The light around the pictures?

Dr. Nanji: Yes, I do.

Annie: I do little things you know? To try to tell you I am there.

Communication 6 ~ Dr. Nanji has an extra session with Leslie Flint because the recorder wasn't turned on for a session. He assumes Annie will be surprised to see him at the extra session, but she says she was with him and two friends, Jim and Elsie Ellis, when they discovered the tape was blank. Listen at www.afterlifeinstitute.org/blank/.

Transcript of an excerpt of the recording:

Dr. Nanji: Yes, Darling … uh … this is a surprise for you?

Annie: Well, not exactly … well, I would not call it a surprise.

Dr. Nanji: No.

Annie: No, because I was very aware of it, you know, when you was with Jimmy …

Dr. Nanji: Yes, yes …

Annie:	and Elsie.
Dr. Nanji:	Yes.
Annie:	and you put this thing [tape] on the machine, you know? And, uh, you were so upset about it …
Dr. Nanji:	Yes, I was. I couldn't sleep …

Communication 7 ~ Annie asks Dr. Nanji why he goes to the cemetery. She says she is not there. The only time she goes there is when he does. She sees him putting flowers on the grave. Listen at www.afterlifeinstitute.org/cemetery/.

Transcript of an excerpt of the recording:

Annie:	Why do you still go to the cemetery?
Dr. Nanji:	Well Darling, how can I pass your birthday without my …
Annie:	I appreciate it, but I'm not there! I'm not there!
Dr. Nanji:	No, no, I know that!
Annie:	And, uh, I see you go there and it makes you depressed.
Dr. Nanji:	Yeah I – no, no, I am not depressed darling.
Annie:	No?
Dr. Nanji:	No, no, no. I am not depressed.
Annie:	And the flowers.
Dr. Nanji:	But the fact that I have cleaned it up and … and I put the bushes round …
Annie:	I know. I see you. I watch you do it and I think …

Dr. Nanji:	Yes. I was there, I was there a week ago.
Annie:	The only time I am ever in the cemetery is when you go there.

Communication 8 ~ Annie says she was with Dr. Nanji all day the day before when he went to visit Gladys Hayter, a medium friend of Dr. Nanji. Annie remarks that Gladys's husband Bert was not there because he had no interest in the idea of spirit pictures. Annie also knew that Dr. Nanji would be going back the day of this recording. Listen at www.afterlifeinstitute.org/gladys/.

Transcript of an excerpt of the recording:

Annie:	I was with you all day yesterday.
Dr. Nanji:	Yes? It was very nice.
Annie:	It was very kind, you know. She is very good you know and she does everything for you.
Dr. Nanji:	Exactly, yes.
Annie:	and the cake and everything.
Dr. Nanji:	She sends her love to you.
Annie:	I know. I will be talking to her, I hope, again.
Dr. Nanji:	…and she took about ten pictures while I was with her.
Annie:	But the pictures. I did pose.
Annie:	Good. You are going back today, are you not?
Dr. Nanji:	Yes, I'm going back.
Annie:	I shall be with you.

Communication 9 ~ In this recording, Annie says she went on the plane with Dr. Nanji to a lunch meeting. She sat close to him. She asked about the several tape recorders in the room. Dr. Nanji explained that the hotel provided them, and they were not all used at once. He supposed the extra tape recorders were in case one was out of order. Listen at www.afterlifeinstitute.org/lunch/.

Transcript of the recording:

Annie: I was with you when you went to the seaside place.

Dr. Nanji: Yes, Darling...

Annie: I was with you in the plane

Dr. Nanji: Yes.

Annie: And I was with you when you had lunch.

Dr. Nanji: Yes.

Annie: And when you were listening to them and the tapes. And you were talking about all sorts of things.

Dr. Nanji: I sat there...

Annie: I was very close to you. What a wonderful arrangement in all this. How many tape recorders have they got in that room?

Dr. Nanji: I think the hotel wrote... But they can only use one.

Annie: Uh huh.

Dr. Nanji: Yes.

Annie: Why?

Dr. Nanji: Well, they did not have all those tape recorders going all the time.

Annie: Oh no, no, I see what you mean.

Dr. Nanji: So I suppose if one is out of order I think they can always have another.

Communication 10 ~ Annie remarks that Dr. Nanji saw a woman as he walked to Flint's office who reminded him of Annie. She explains that he almost stopped and had a feeling "as if your heart stopped beating." She then describes his thoughts: "She was very like me. Also the way she moved, walked, you know." She was able to register Dr. Nanji's thoughts and sentiments, demonstrating the mind-to-mind communication expected when a person on earth communicates with a person living in spirit. Listen at www.afterlifeinstitute.org/woman/.

Transcript for an excerpt of the recording:

Annie: You know the other day ...

Dr. Nanji: Yeah?

Annie: ...before you come here?

Dr. Nanji: Yes.

Annie: You were walking along the street ...

Dr. Nanji: Yes?

Annie: ...and you saw someone in the distance and it reminded you of me.

Dr. Nanji: [Laughing] Oh, correct!

Annie:	And for a moment you almost stopped, you know. As if your heart stopped beating.
Dr. Nanji:	Yes!
Annie:	But you knew it was not me, in a way, but …
Dr. Nanji:	Yes, of course.
Annie:	…at the same time, she was very like me.
Dr. Nanji:	Yes.
Annie:	Also the way she moved … walked, you know? Ah, but this of course is …
Dr. Nanji:	And do you know, I, I thought mentally "Yes, it looks like her, but she hasn't got her brain!"

Additional recordings of Annie Nanji communicating from spirit to her husband are at www.afterlifeinstitute.org/annie/.

Annie Nanji's Conversations with Dr. Nanji after Her Body's Death Add to the Evidence We Live On after the Body Dies

The conversations demonstrate that Annie was alive and mentally capable, with fully functioning senses, a functioning memory, the ability to observe Dr. Nanji in his daily life, and recollections of their life together, years after her body had died. They demonstrate that Annie is alive after her body died, just as you will be when your body dies.

2. Alice Fearon Communicates with Her Son in Spirit

Summary

In 1944, Michael Rodney Fearon was killed in World War II. His mother came to Leslie Flint and spoke to Michael repeatedly beginning in 1954. Three recordings of the conversations exist. The fact that Mrs. Fearon came repeatedly and had intimate conversations with her son is evidence that Michael continued to live after his body ceased to function.

Michael Rodney Fearon

Michael Rodney Fearon was born November 30, 1916, to Frank and Alice Fearon in Mayfield, Sussex, England. According to the archivist at Taunton School, Somerset, Michael Fearon joined the faculty in September 1938 and taught biology for two years until he was called to serve in World War II.

U.K. military records show that Michael Fearon, service number 91828, was a captain in "The Buffs" (Royal East Kent Regiment). He was killed in action June 24, 1944, at age 27. A staff register at Taunton School states that he "died of wounds." His body was buried at Banneville-la-Campagne War Cemetery in France.

Alice Fearon

Michael's mother, Alice Fearon, regularly visited Leslie Flint on Fridays to speak with her son whose body had died. Three recordings of these sessions exist, from 1954, 1966, and 1969. They contain casual conversations between a mother and her son in spirit. Michael's body had been dead for at least ten years when the conversations took place.

The Evidence Demonstrating Michael Fearon Is Alive and Well Although His Body Was Killed on the Battlefield

The excerpt below is from a recording made in 1954. Alice Fearon certified that she had been speaking with her son. You can listen to the recording at www.afterlifeinstitute.org/fearon/.

Transcript of the recording:

Michael: Satisfactory. I mean, I love coming to talk to you; it's a wonderful opportunity and it means so much to me, as indeed it does to everybody who has the opportunity to come through and speak to those who they love on earth.

Mrs. Fearon: I know …

Michael: It would make such a vast difference to people if they understood this and realize that death isn't what they think it is. It isn't the separation of contact between us.

Mrs. Fearon: There is no death, is there? There is no death.

Michael: It's only an illusion. Man has created death in his own mind.

On October 8, 1963, the BBC arranged a broadcast during which they played this recording. The commentator, Peter Williams, asked Alice Fearon whether the recording was of her son. This is the transcript of the BBC interview.

Peter Williams: That was a conversation between a mother and her son. A tape recording, as a matter of fact, made in a room something like this one here. … But the recording was taken eleven years after the son died, killed in action three weeks after the D-Day landings in Normandy in France, during the last war. But throughout Britain there are thousands of people who believe implicitly in the authenticity of this conversation, and others like it — talks between the living and the dead. But what about the woman most directly concerned in this conversation? What does **she** think about this? Mrs. Fearon, as Mike's mother, what makes you so sure that it's your son's voice that you can hear?

Mrs. Fearon: Well, Mike was twenty-seven when he died and I'd been with him all that time. They were day boys for a long time, and they were my life, and I ought to know at the end of that, oughtn't I?

Peter Williams: The voice on the tape recorder and the voice you remember, are they very similar?

Mrs. Fearon: Yes.

Peter Williams: The same pitch, the same inflections?

Mrs. Fearon: Just about.[2]

Michael Fearon's Conversations with His Mother after His Body's Death Prove You Will Never Die

The recordings are of Michael Fearon in spirit speaking to his mother, demonstrating that he was alive and mentally capable, with all fully functioning senses, a functioning memory, and recollections of their life together, years after his body had died.

3. Eira Conacher Communicates with Her Husband, Douglas, Living in the Life after This Life

Summary

Eira Conacher spoke in Leslie Flint sessions with her husband living in the life after this life, Douglas Conacher. The conversational quality of the sessions and her repeated visits are evidence she was certain she was conversing with her husband, whose body had died years before.

Douglas Conacher

Douglas had served in World War I and was greatly affected by the war because of his sensitive nature. Years of illness, operations, and frustrations followed. It became necessary for him to give up his publishing business in the heart of London and try to find rest and peace in rural surroundings.

Douglas was deeply religious and a devout member of the Church of England. The books he published were chiefly on orthodox religion and philosophy. He had an overwhelming love of books and read widely, but nothing of a psychic or occult nature.[3]

Eira Conacher

Douglas and Eira did not meet until rather late in life. Douglas was 58 and a confirmed bachelor. Eira was 39 and deeply involved in her work as art mistress in a school in Surrey, outside London. On August 12, 1937, a few months after a chance meeting, the two were married.[4]

The Evidence Demonstrating People Transition from the Body but Do Not Die

Eira Conacher visited Leslie Flint over 40 times from 1965 through 1967, usually at intervals of two or three weeks, producing twenty-three recordings. Eira and Douglas carried on regular conversations and authored two books together: *There Is Life after Death: Tape Recordings from the Other World*[5] and *Chapters of Experience.*[6] It is apparent from the intimate conversations that Eira, living on earth, was having normal conversations with her husband, Douglas, after his body had died.

You can listen to part of a recording made in 1965, seven years after Douglas passed. Flint and Eira were the only ones in the room. In the recording, Eira speaks first. The recording is at www.afterlifeinstitute.org/conachers/.

Transcript of the recording:

Eira: Was that your light I saw last night?

Douglas: Yes. You know, I'm wondering if you do see as much as I hope you do. I try to attract your attention in various ways and I felt sure... in fact, the other evening, I felt sure you realized I was there. You do sense my presence even though you don't see me.

Eira: Yes.

Douglas: You know, sometimes during your sleep you come here... and we're together.

Eira: Yes.

Douglas: We're together a great deal, you know.

Eira: Really? I wish I could remember. I have occasionally remembered.

Douglas: Yes. Have you decided to stay as you are or what? Are you thinking of making a change?

Eira: Well, you tell me to remain where I am at the moment.

Douglas: Well yes, that's what I think. I think you would be well advised to stay put and not to make any change for the moment. I don't think there would be much point and it would not be a good idea to do anything drastic.

Eira: Well, I have so many interests.

Douglas: I don't know...

Eira: Yes. Darling, I haven't asked after your favorite cat lately.

Douglas: Oh, he's very well.

Eira: How's he getting on?

Douglas:	He's fine. You know I do love my animals.
Eira:	I know. You did love that cat very much.
Douglas:	Not as much as I love you!
Eira:	No. Well, I'm awfully glad you still love me.
Douglas:	Of course I do! I always shall. I'm just waiting for the day for you to join me.
Eira:	Yes.
Douglas:	The years come and go. Time will pass and we shall be together.
Eira:	That will be lovely.

Eira Conacher's Conversations with Douglas after His Body's Death Prove You Will Never Die

The recordings of Douglas in spirit speaking to his wife, Eira, demonstrate that he was alive and mentally capable with fully functioning senses, a functioning memory, and recollections of their life together, years after his body had died. Douglas was aware of current events in Eira's life, demonstrating that he continues to live, with keen, functioning senses and memory.

4. David Cattanach Communicates with His Mother in Sessions with Leslie Flint

Summary

A young man named David Cattanach, whose body died at age eighteen, made many visits to the Leslie Flint séances over a period of ten years, speaking with his mother at several of them.

Mrs. Cattanach

Gordon Smith, the well-known British psychic medium who knew David's mother personally, wrote this about her and the sessions during which she spoke with her son:

> I know her personally and she is someone I would describe as very astute, someone who would not easily be fooled, especially when it came to her son, and she had no doubts that she was hearing his voice.[7]

The Evidence Demonstrating That David Is Alive Although His Body Is Dead

Following is a brief excerpt of Mrs. Cattanach speaking with her son in a Leslie Flint direct-voice session. Listen to this recording at www.afterlifeinstitute.org/cattanach/.

Transcript of the recording:

Mrs. Cattanach: Is Bob working with you?

David: Yes. We're very close because we house together.

Mrs. Cattanach: Oh, that's lovely.

David: We do a great deal of work together as a matter of fact.

Mrs. Cattanach: And Darling, is Tom with you still?

David: Yes, yes.

Mrs. Cattanach: Good.

David: I say, can you hear me?

Mrs. Cattanach: Yes, very well, Dear.

Evidence from Direct-Voice Mediumship Proves You Will Never Die

These people who lived normal lives on earth left their bodies behind to go on to the life after this life. They were able to return to earth to converse through direct-voice mediums with people who knew them well. They carried on casual conversations as they did when they were using bodies. The people on earth accepted these conversations as valid because they recognized the person in spirit's unique voice quality, personality, references to current events, and reminiscences of past events in the people's lives.

They did not die when their bodies died. The communication through direct-voice mediums is evidence you will never die.

Chapter 2

Communication through Materialization Mediumship Is Evidence You Will Never Die

Sitters in séances with materialization mediums experience having people known to them materialize and address them directly. The sitters verify that the people materializing are the individuals they knew when they were in bodies on the earth plane. The statements by the people now in spirit demonstrate that they know the sitters personally and are aware of events that occurred after their bodies died, including very recent events.

1. A Man Whose Body Is Dead Speaks to His Love

Summary

During a séance with materialization medium David Thompson, a man named Nick came through to speak to one of the sitters, Sarah.

David Thompson

David Thompson conducts séances in darkened rooms with direct voices and materializations of those in spirit in the presence of a variety of people with careful, rigid controls. These include inspections by more than one sitter, before the séances begin, of a gag across his mouth and zip ties binding his body to a chair. You can listen to descriptions of David Thompson's séances verified by four witnesses and read four research articles about his séances at www.afterlifeinstitute.org/david/.

Evidence Demonstrating People Continue to Live On after Their Bodies and Brains Die

In one recorded séance with David Thompson, a man named Nick, whose body had died, materialized and spoke to Sarah, his beloved companion, who was among the sitters. Speaking using the ectoplasmic voice box is very difficult for people in spirit. They must impress their thoughts on it in a manner that results in audible words. Nick was not familiar with speaking through the ectoplasm, so he spoke in a whisper because he could not activate the ectoplasmic vocal cords. Sarah has graciously agreed to allow us to share her experience to demonstrate the reality of survival of consciousness.

You can listen to this reunion between Sarah and Nick at www.afterlifeinstitute.org/sarah-nick/, where Nick speaks from spirit through the ectoplasmic vocal mechanism.

Transcript of Sarah communicating with Nick:

Nick: Can you hear me?

All: Yes we can hear you. You're OK. Yes, you're OK. You're fine.

Nick: Oh my God. I'm a bit frightened of this.

All: It's all right. You're OK. You're amongst friends. You're OK. Just remain calm. Just relax. It's OK.

Keith: It's just a bit strange.

Nick: You're right. It is strange.

All: It is strange. But it's all right.

Keith: Take a moment to adjust.

Nick: Never thought I'd do this.

Wendy: It's wonderful that you have.

Keith: Can you tell us who you are?

Nick: My name's Nick.

All: It's Nick. Hello Nick. Hi Nick.

Sarah: Baby.

Nick: I can't. Sarah, I want to see Sarah.

All: You're here to see Sarah.

Sarah: Darling, I'm here.

Rosheen: Sarah, speak up to him.

Sarah: Nick...

Nick: Can you hear me?

Sarah: Yeah I can, Darling. I love you, baby. I love you so much.

Nick: I love you, too.

Sarah: Don't ever leave me OK. I know you're with me.

Nick:	I spend as much time with you as I can. I'm always gonna be there.
Sarah:	OK, my baby, just stay close. I love you so much and you know how grateful I am to you for doing this.
Nick:	You know something, all those things that you've bought?
Sarah:	Yeah.
Nick:	At the cottage, they're just lost. They're lost.
Sarah:	Yeah?
Nick:	Don't worry about them.
Sarah:	Really?
Nick:	I knew you was there. I knew you was there.
Sarah:	Did you, Darling? I do, I just, was I enough for you? I just...
Nick:	Listen to me, listen to me. We haven't got long. Listen to me.
Sarah:	OK, my baby.
Nick:	Always remember...
Sarah:	Yeah?
Nick:	I love you with all my heart.

Sarah: OK.

Nick: I told you that just before I left you.

Sarah: I know.

Nick: I'll always be with you. I'll always be with you.

Sarah: OK, my Darling.

Nick: Promise me something. I want you to be happy.

Sarah: I will for you. I will for you. I'll make the best of what I've got here. For you.

Nick: Remember whatever happens we'll always be together before we meet again.

Sarah: You promise me that?

Nick: I promise you.

Sarah: You...

Nick: From the bottom of my heart, I promise you.

Sarah: OK, my Darling.

Nick: I want you to be happy.

Sarah: I will try. I am trying I'm trying so hard. It's just such a shock you know. But I'm trying hard. I'm doing better, I'm doing better, Darling.

Nick: You are, girl, and you're doing fantastic.

Sarah:	As long as I've got you with me and I know I do. I just hope I did enough for you.
Nick:	Yes, you did. You were everything I ever wanted.
Sarah:	I was? Good. I just wanted to be enough.
Nick:	That's why I died peacefully.
Sarah:	You... oh thank goodness.
Nick:	That's why I had that look of peace on my face.
Sarah:	Yes. Did you see me when I went to see you?
Nick:	Yes, I did. And everything you put into the coffin. I saw it all.
Sarah:	Oh, thank you, Darling. I tried to do right by you. I tried to do everything I could. I really tried hard.
Nick:	You done for me what a man could ever want. More than any man could ever want.
Sarah:	OK, my baby, because you know you were worth it. You don't ever doubt how much I loved you and how much I will continue to love you. Don't ever doubt it.
Nick:	Don't ever doubt my love for you.
Sarah:	OK, my baby.
	[Nick places his hands around Sarah's face in an embrace]

Oh!! Oh I love you. I love you.

[The "whooshing" sound of dematerialization]

Keith: You OK, Sarah?

Sarah: Yeah

Keith & Chris: Good.

Sarah's Communication with Nick Contributes to the Evidence That We Live On after the Body Dies

Sarah had no doubt that the materialized man who stood before her and spoke to her was her deceased love, Nick. She carried on an extended conversation with him about things the two knew intimately. During the conversation, it was clear that Nick was alive even though his body had died. He referred to things that happened during their lives together before his transition and to events that occurred after the transition that Sarah was clearly relieved about.

2. Konstantin Raudive Materializes and Speaks to Sonia Rinaldi

Summary

During one of materialization medium David Thompson's séances in 2014, Konstantin Raudive, whose body had been dead since 1974, materialized and spoke to Brazilian instrumental transcommunication researcher Sonia Rinaldi. In instrumental transcommunication, people whose bodies have died cause their voices to be recorded on audio recorders, their images to appear on televisions or monitors, or their images to appear on surfaces such as fabrics that are video recorded. In his message, Raudive revealed that he knew of Rinaldi's current research and made a suggestion for improving it.

Konstantin Raudive

Konstantin Raudive, a Latvian psychologist who studied under psychoanalyst Carl Jung, was the first researcher in instrumental transcommunication to diligently record voices of people living in the life after this life. Beginning in 1965, Raudive recorded 72,000 distinct voices.[8] He is acknowledged as the foremost early pioneer in instrumental transcommunication.

Sonia Rinaldi

The most active, groundbreaking instrumental transcommunication researcher in the world today is Sonia Rinaldi of Brazil. Sonia creates new methods and devices that are continually improving the recordings of voices and images of people living in the life after this life. The speakers converse with her and show their awareness of what she is doing.

During a David Thompson séance, a man announcing himself as Konstantin Raudive materialized and spoke to Sonia. Raudive's reference to Sonia's work and how she could improve the results demonstrates that he was alive, aware of her work, and anxious to continue working with her from spirit. This recording is available at www.afterlifeinstitute.org/raudive/.

Sonia has difficulty understanding him, so Sheri Perl and Victor Zammit, sitting next to her, repeat what Raudive has said. Raudive refers to Sonia's images of people in spirit she records on video. Mickey, Leslie Flint's companion who brings through people in Flint's séances, speaks at the beginning. Sonia refers to a phone call Raudive made to her from spirit. You can listen to the recording of the event at https://afterlifeinstitute.org/raudive/.

Transcript of the recording:

Sonia: Yes?

Mickey: Is your name Sonia?

Sonia: Yes.

Mickey: There is a man here that wants to speak to you.

Sonia: Oh...

Mickey: His name is, hold on... Oh he wants to tell you his name himself.

Sonia: Thank you!

Raudive: Sonia, Sonia Rinaldi.

Sonia: Yes.

Raudive: My name is Konstantin Raudive.

Sonia: Oh. Mr. Raudive. Thank you for your presence. Thank you.

Raudive: I want you to know that I am working with you a lot of the time.

Sheri Perl repeats for Sonia.

Sonia: Oh, thank you. I am sorry. Sometimes I don't understand quite well. But Sheri is helping me.

Raudive: I want you to know that there is a problem with the communication.

Sonia: Yes, is there anything that I can do?

Raudive: Yes.

Sonia: Sure! Please tell me.

Raudive: You need...

Sonia: Yes.

Raudive:	to create a symmetric current path between two capacitors.

Sheri Perl repeats for Sonia.

Sonia:	Yes. If you can help me to reach this, I will try all the way.
Raudive:	I will try. I will bring word through your communication channels. And I will help you. And we will accomplish many things together.
Sonia:	OK thank you. Thank you. I will do anything that I can.
Raudive:	Yes, I know and that is why I come to work with you often.
Sonia:	Oh, thank you so much.
Raudive:	I thank you.
Sonia:	You know that I call you Mr. German, right?
Raudive:	You can call me what you wish.
Sonia:	Oh, thank you!
Raudive:	Have you seen my face yet?

Victor Zammit repeats for Sonia.

Raudive:	I will appear on your communication.
Sonia:	Oh!
Raudive:	You will see me on your images, yes.

Konstantin Raudive's Conversation with Sonia Rinaldi Contributes to the Evidence That We Live On after the Body Dies

Konstantin Raudive materialized and stood before Sonia Rinaldi, speaking to her about her work using a technical explanation he knew would be helpful to her. He had been working with her in her instrumental transcommunication for several years. Sonia called him "Mr. German" because for a period of time she just heard a man with a German accent speaking to her, without knowing it was Raudive. His presence and fluent conversation about things current in Sonia's life are evidence he lives on although his body has died, proving you will live on also when your body dies.

3. Carlos Mirabelli Produces Two Materializations of Individuals before Witnesses

Summary

Brazilian medium Carlos Mirabelli enabled the materialization of individuals living on the next plane of life in daylight before a variety of assembled witnesses. The following recounts the materialization of a man's daughter and an esteemed physician. Assembled were highly qualified, competent physicians and scientists who attested to the reality of the experiences.

Carlos Mirabelli

Brazilian materialization medium Carlos Mirabelli's talents are difficult to catalogue exhaustively. He engaged in automatic writing in twenty-eight languages, three of which are dead (Latin, Chaldean, and hieroglyphics), and spoke in two during medium sessions. He was responsible for physical mediumship phenomena, such as levitation of objects and himself, transportation of objects, dematerialization of organic and inorganic objects, luminous appearances, and rapping and other sounds. He experienced the materializations of complete human beings in broad daylight. His remarkable abilities were tested under rigorous conditions.[9]

Evidence Demonstrating People Transition but Do Not Die

The Cesar Lombroso Academy of Psychic Studies, founded to study Mirabelli's mediumistic activities, reported a materialization that occurred in broad daylight in a room of about 1,000 square meters, with stone walls and locked doors. After three knocks a voice called "Papa." One of the researchers present was Dr. Ganymede de Souza. He said he recognized the voice as his recently deceased daughter. The figure of the young girl materialized. Weeping, Dr. de Souza embraced the fully materialized

Daughter of Dr. Ganymede de Souza standing behind Mirabelli

girl. He reported that she was wearing the same dress in which she had been buried. A physician present, Colonel Octavio Viana, took the child in his arms, felt her pulse, and asked her several questions, which she answered with understanding. After thirty-six minutes of communication, the child floated around in the air and disappeared.[10]

Although her body had died, the girl fully materialized and spoke to the sitters, including her father.

In another instance, at 2 p.m. in daylight, the deceased German teacher Dr. George Zencker materialized. Nandor Fodor, a lawyer who was the London correspondent for the American

Society for Psychical Research (ASPR), reported on the incident for the ASPR.

At that séance Mirabelli was in trance when a bell on the table levitated and started to ring. It woke Mirabelli, who then described a man he had seen clairvoyantly. As he spoke, the man began to materialize.

Two sitters recognized him as the deceased Dr. Zencker, whom they knew. A physician present tried to examine the apparition, but it floated away. As Fodor said, "the figure began to dissolve from the feet upwards, the bust and arms floating in the air."[11]

The materialization had the upper-eyelid ptosis Dr. Zencker had in his right eye. Witnesses were Dr. Alencar de Macedo (who took the photograph), Dr. João de Azevedo Braga, Dr. Felisberto Marcondes, Dr. Horacio de Souza, and Dr. Honorio de Macedo.[12]

Materialization of Dr. George Zencker

Materializations of the Little Girl and Dr. Zencker Contribute to the Evidence That You Will Never Die

The materialization of the little girl was photographed and attested to by her father and the assembled researchers. She was alive and able to communicate, although her body had died.

The materialization of Dr. Zencker took place before reliable witnesses and was photographed. He was identifiable by his upper-eyelid ptosis.

The two reports with photographs were filed with the Cesar Lombroso Academy of Psychic Studies.

4. Helen Duncan's Trial Witnesses Confirm the Materializations of People They Know Intimately

Helen Duncan was a twentieth-century British materialization medium. During one of her séances in 1941 a sailor came through, explaining he had perished when the HMS Barham was sunk. The British Admiralty, worried about public morale, had been keeping the incident secret. Some two years later, as D-Day approached, they wanted to prevent any further revelations. Duncan was arrested and tried under the Witchcraft Act of 1735. The Admiralty's reaction to her knowledge demonstrated that they knew her statements were accurate.

Helen Duncan's trial began on March 30, 1944. Twenty-two witnesses described the connections they had made during Duncan's séances with loved ones in spirit. Following are brief transcripts of five sworn testimonies focusing on three areas of evidence for survival of consciousness:

- The witnesses experienced the materializations of people with whom they had intimate relationships, such as parents, children, and spouses.

- The witnesses asserted that the materialized individuals had all the physical and mental characteristics of the people they knew when they were on earth.

- The witnesses described the occasions when the person in spirit spoke about events after the death of their bodies, showing they were still alive and mentally capable, with fully functioning memories.

All are demonstrations that people live on, fully functioning and aware, after their bodies have died.

Transcripts of portions of the five testimonies follow. No original audio recordings are available, but the links with each witness's testimony go to a narrations of the testimonies. Links to full transcripts of all twenty-two witnesses are at www.afterlifeinstitute.org/witnesses/.

Witness: *Jane Mary Rust*

Jane Mary Rust, a municipal midwife nurse, testified at the Old Bailey Central Criminal Court in London during Duncan's trial. She swore under oath that her reports of her experiences conversing with her deceased husband, mother, and aunt were true. As the materialized people came very near to her, touched her, and allowed her to touch them, they showed all the physical, mental, and memory characteristics of the people she knew.

Excerpts from the trial testimony follow.[13] You can read this testimony while listening to a narration at www.afterlifeinstitute.org/jane/.

> **Defense Attorney:** Had you any doubt about it being your husband?
>
> **Jane Rust:** No doubt whatsoever.
>
> **Defense Attorney:** How close up to him were you?
>
> **Jane Rust:** As close as I am to this.
>
> **Defense Attorney:** Did he speak to you?
>
> **Jane Rust:** He spoke to me.
>
> **Defense Attorney:** Did you recognize his voice?

Jane Rust: I did. I was perfectly certain.

Defense Attorney: Did he say anything to you in particular that struck you as of importance?

Jane Rust: Just spoke about the family. He said that he was always with me, and he would be on the other side waiting for me; he would never leave me until I joined him.

Defense Attorney: Had he altered in appearance at all?

Jane Rust: No, sir, he had not altered just a wee bit thinner, perhaps, than he was in health, but my husband was very ill for three years before he went.

Jane Rust: He said, "Put your hand in mine, dear," so I gave him my right hand. He took hold of it with his right and clasped my hand very tightly.

Judge: It was flesh and blood, was it?

Jane Rust: It was very cold, my Lord, but it was his hand. I held it firmly. I felt the knuckles. He suffered with rheumatism, my Lord, and I felt the nobbly knuckles.

Defense Attorney: Did he kiss you?

Jane Rust: He did, sir, right on the mouth....

> [My mother] came out and stood on the side of the cabinet. I wanted to be close to her, because I had never been so close before; I wanted to get right in contact. I said, "Mother, you are not going back without kissing me, are you, this time?" She said, "Come here, my child"; she beckoned me to her side. She made me stand, and I was standing facing her. She turned me to the sitters and patted

my shoulder and said, "My loving daughter" introduced me, sort of thing.

Defense Attorney: Did you touch her?

Jane Rust: I did. I kissed her.

Defense Attorney: Did she put her arms on you, or did you put your arms on her?

Jane Rust: She put her arm around my shoulders.

Defense Attorney: Tell me a little about her voice. What was her voice like?

Jane Rust: It was her natural voice....

> My mother had a mole in the hollow of her chin and another over the left eyebrow, and without that it would not be my mother, and she had it there, and I was satisfied....
>
> I got as close to [my aunt] as I got to my mother and my husband....
>
> She said to me [words in Spanish here]. I said [words in Spanish]....
>
> It was Gibraltarian Spanish. It was not the Spanish, possibly, that they speak in Spain itself, but the Gibraltarian Spanish.

Defense Attorney: Did you recognize the figure that spoke to you?

Jane Rust: Yes, absolutely, sir. She was my aunt, my mother's sister, and I recognized her because she is a replica of my own mother; they were always taken for twins, but they were not twins.

Witness: James McDougal Duncan

James McDougal Duncan, a jeweler unrelated to Helen Duncan, testified under oath at her trial. He and his daughter had experiences and dialogue showing his materialized wife was alive although her body was dead. She exhibited

- All the physical, mental, and memory characteristics known to him and his daughter as she came near to them
- Her mental and sensory awareness when she referred to a trip to Canada the family had been discussing just prior to the séance

Excerpts from the trial testimony follow.[14] You can listen to a narration of the testimony as you read it at www.afterlifeinstitute.org/james-duncan/.

Mr. Duncan: [my wife] went to the side next the light and pulled the curtain aside and stood there with the light shining clear on her face. I went up to her and saw her. I was within eighteen inches of her. I spoke to her. I saw her most clearly, the best I have ever seen her.

Defense Attorney: What did she say? Do you remember?

Mr. Duncan: Intimate things. We have discussed certain intimate and domestic things. She knew that we had considered going to Canada to my son there, and she told me at the sitting there once, "Go to Canada. You will be much happier. You will be in better health. Go there."

Defense Attorney: What about the voice? Was it her voice?

Mr. Duncan: My wife's voice.

Defense Attorney: What about the appearance?

Mr. Duncan: Yes, the appearance of my wife. I lived with her forty-five years; I should know her voice and her appearance.... I have not a shadow of doubt in my mind that the form I saw was that of my wife, speaking to me, as she used to speak, in a quiet voice. She had a quiet voice.

Defense Attorney: How close to you did [your father] come?

Mr. Duncan: I went right up to the cabinet and spoke to him.... Because I knew my father. He had a beard and spoke in the voice that I knew well. He was just about my height....

I went right up to the curtain too, and [my mother] spoke to me. She said, "Are those the lassies?" My two daughters were there. I said, "Yes." She said, "It makes me feel old." Now that is just what she would have said had she been on the earth, just the very same expression she would have used.

Defense Attorney: How do you know it was your mother at all?

Mr. Duncan: By seeing her and hearing her. I saw her quite clearly. I was quite close to her.

Defense Attorney: You recognized your brothers?

Mr. Duncan: Yes.

Defense Attorney: By appearance and voice?

Mr. Duncan: Yes.

Defense Attorney: No doubt about it at all?

Mr. Duncan: Not at all. Not at all.

Witness: Alfred Dodd

Alfred Dodd, a historian, senior Freemason, and acclaimed author of works on Shakespeare's sonnets, testified at Helen Duncan's trial that in her séances his grandfather, mother, and first sweetheart had materialized and spoken to him.

He had experiences and dialogue showing the people who materialized were alive although their bodies were dead. In their materializations, Dodd was able to confirm

- All the physical characteristics of the person he knew as his materialized grandfather:
    - "A very big man."
    - "A very tall man, about 6 feet 1 at least, very corpulent."
    - "He had on his smoking-cap that he used to wear. He was dressed in a dark suit. He had on the donkey fringe I knew so well, having been brought up with him since five years of age."
    - "His face was brown and bronzed, just in the same way; the same look in his eye; the same expression and tones that I knew so well."
- All the physical characteristics of his childhood sweetheart, Helen:
    - The same hair that I knew so well, dark and ruddy; the same eyes, hazel; they shone with animation; her face, the same ivory pallor on her cheeks."
- All his grandfather's mental and memory characteristics:
    - "He spoke just as if he was one of the family."

- - "... he then continued and said, 'Ban is here.' Ban, that is the pet name for the old nurse that I used to have as a child, which I had known as I grew up."
  - "He said, 'Keep your pecker up, old boy.' That was one of his characteristic expressions."
- Helen's vocal characteristics:
  - "Then I heard her speak, and she spoke in the same soft Scotch accent that I knew so well."
  - "... it was a cultured Scotch, not a harsh Glasgow Scotch, nothing like it not harsh at all; a soft cultured voice, mixed, of course, with her training in England educationally."
- His grandfather's knowledge of Dodd's present life when he referred to Dodd's financial difficulties and that Dodd was editing a volume of Shakespeare's sonnets

Excerpts from his trial testimony follow, uninterrupted by statements and questions.[15] You can listen to a narration of the testimony as you read it at www.afterlifeinstitute.org/alfred/.

Alfred Dodd: The curtains went on one side, and out there came the living form of my grandfather. I knew it was him, because he was a very big man.... A very tall man, about 6ft. 1 at least, very corpulent. He looked round the room very quizzically until his eyes caught mine. He then strode across the room from the seance cabinet to where I was. He pushed the heads of the two strangers that were before me on one side like that, and he put out his hand and he grasped mine. He said as he grasped it, "I am very pleased to see you, Alfred, here in my native city."

I was very surprised at seeing him, and I looked at him most closely, and I said to him, "Why, you look just the same."

He had on his smoking-cap that he used to wear. He was dressed in a dark suit. He had on the donkey fringe I knew so well, having been brought up with him since five years of age. His face was brown and bronzed, just in the same way; the same look in his eye; the same expression and tones that I knew so well. As a matter of fact, he was born in Manchester, and I was born in Manchester....

He next said, "I am sorry you are having such a rough time." I was, because I was losing a lot of money on property at that time, and he seemed to know all about it. He spoke just as if he was one of the family. He touched on something very private and personal, which I could not make mention of in this court very well, but he then continued and said, "Ban is here." Ban, that is the pet name for the old nurse that I used to have as a child, which I had known as I grew up. "Ban is here." I said, "I am very glad. I hope you are getting on very well." He said, "Keep your pecker up, old boy" that was one of his characteristic expressions; "Never say die while there is a shot in the locker."

He was holding my hand all the time. He held it with so firm a grip that my hand ached for hours afterwards. There was thrown over him, as it were, a net of I should think half-inch mesh; there seemed to be thrown over him a net, because, as I held his hand, I pulled the net in my hand quite distinctly. He stepped back like that and he put his hand on my friend's shoulder, who was sitting at the front. He put his hand on and clapped him on the shoulder and said, "Stand up, Tom," just in the same commanding way he used to speak. "Stand up, Tom"... So Tom Wallace stood up and, when he stood up, my grandfather being a much bigger man than him in every way, he said, "Look into my face, and look into my eyes." He said, "Will you know me again, Mr. Wallace?" Wallace said, "Yes." "Very good. You ask Albert tomorrow to show you my portrait, which is hanging on the wall in his dining-room, and you will see it is the same man as is speaking to you, now."

He turned round and walked back to the cabinet, and he lifted up his leg and he slapped his thigh three times, three loud resounding smacks, and then he went right to the curtain and he lifted himself to his full height. He smote himself on the breast three times, so that everybody could hear. He said, "It is solid, Alfred; it is solid," and he went away inside. That was the first personal experience I had....

He said before he went, I ought to add to my evidence, one more remarkable thing. He said, "You are on the right track, Alfred. Go on with your work," he said, "I mean the sonnets," and there was not a living person in Manchester who knew I was interested in Shakespeare's sonnets. I was editing an edition of Shakespeare's sonnets....

After the voice had come and several forms had come out to other people, he [Albert, Duncan's control] called out and said, "There is a lady here, an old lady who wants a gentleman in the front row, and she is calling out the name of Jim." Now I saw a little old body come out, very small in a dark garment, white of face, grey hair, and I recognized her by her photograph.... She came out without the slightest hesitation, and came straight from the cabinet, through the curtains right to where Mr. James Waller was sitting in the front row, and as she seized his hand and as he took hers, I heard the two. I heard the two voices. He said, "Oh, mother, mother," and she said to him, "My boy, my boy." They had a private conversation. I took the place of the sister who ought to have been there, and that was referred to in the course of the conversation.

She was very, very sorry a sister, a girl named Lily, was poorly. Then he said, "My brother Tom is here, you know." She said, "Yes, I am going to him," and she disengaged her hand quite literally, and went across an intervening space of two or three persons and went to shake hands with Tom. As she finished shaking hands with him, she said, "Now, be good to your father," and she went back.

As soon as ever she had gone back into the cabinet, Albert's voice called out once more, and he said that lady's name. We will call her grandmother Mary. He said, "She has brought with her a little girl, and her name is little Mary" we will call her. He said, "Now little Mary has come to look for her daddy and her mummy; they are here." As she spoke, I saw a white formless mist which seemed to come through the curtain; it came through the curtain in such a way that it remained about three yards from the sitters, and this formless mist began to condense. It took shape, and there I saw, to my astonishment, a little girl with a rope in her hand and she was skipping. I can see the twist of her hands even now, it was so real. It went on for six or seven skips, and then this little girl appeared almost to clamber on her knee, and sat between her knees, in some way.

Then the voice of Albert called out, "Come back; come back," but the little girl said, "I want to show them my curls. I want to show them my curls." He said, "You must come at once." She said, "No, I will not." There was quite a little altercation, and the two voices were crossing each other from outside and inside. Then he said, "All right. Show the curls," and she showed her head. I saw them; I saw those golden curls. I was sitting right behind. She bent her head forward, and that was that. Then she went back....

The curtains opened once more, and I saw before me the living form, the living form! of a young lady aged twenty-one. Her name was Helen to me, and she was the first sweetheart that I had ever had, and therefore I knew her. I knew her absolutely. She stood there and she put up her hand to me, and waved in exactly the same way that she waved when I took her to her last social. She stood on the stairs, half-way up, and waved me away. She stood there dressed in a white flowing robe, and over that white flowing robe was a fine curtain of net....

I was so astonished that I stood up in my seat, which I ought not to have done, and I called out to my wife at the other end of the room, and I said to her, "Why, it's Helen; it's Helen." The girl did not come to me direct, she came right round the room from left to right, and she stood before me, a living, palpitating woman. The same hair that I knew so well, dark and ruddy; the same eyes, hazel; they shone with animation; her face, the same ivory pallor on her cheeks....

I said as I looked at her, "Well, I am glad to see you. I am glad. I was only talking about you last night." Then I heard her speak, and she spoke in the same soft Scotch accent that I knew so well.... She came from (unintelligible) but it was a cultured Scotch, not a harsh Glasgow Scotch, nothing like it not harsh at all; a soft cultured voice, mixed, of course, with her training in England educationally, and she was so real as she stood there that night.

Witness: Herbert John Steabben

Herbert John Steabben, a well-known medium, lecturer, and healer who formed the Pathfinders Society, testified that he had witnessed materializations of his mother and a child he knew whose leg had been amputated.

He had experiences and dialogue showing the people who materialized were alive although their bodies were dead. In their materializations they exhibited

- All the physical, mental, and memory characteristics of the people he knew, as they came very near to him and spoke with him
- The mental and sensory awareness of a child who was put in a coffin and materialized after her body had died

Excerpts from his trial testimony follow.[16] You can listen to a narration of the testimony as you read it at www.afterlifeinstitute.org/herbert/.

Herbert Steabben: [My mother] came clearly out from the cabinet and stood about three to four feet clear of the curtains, a full materialization. I noticed the grey hair. I noticed the difference in the eyes. The eyes are grey, whereas Mrs. Duncan's are brown.

> She is about half or one-third the size, and she had the peculiar little mannerisms, that as my mother I naturally recognized.

Defense Attorney: What did she say to you?

Herbert Steabben: She called me by a name other than I have given here as my own name to-day.... She called me Charles.

Defense Attorney: You recognized the voice?

Herbert Steabben: Yes.

Defense Attorney: Did you see your mother's features?

Herbert Steabben: Certainly. I saw the color of her eyes.... She had a little mannerism that, when she was under emotion, one would see before she broke down the lips tremble, like a mother would; and it was very characteristic when she was very stirred. She was stirred naturally then, and I had to comfort her instead of she comforting me....

> This little child of fourteen [who materialized] had long black hair. She had skinny arms, and very shortish, and she was very quick. She had had her leg amputated before she passed into spirit. She came out to show that she had the use of that leg. She was well able to dance, which was a thing she wanted to do when she was in life, but was unable. It was tragic.
>
> She also gave what to me was a wonderful piece of evidence. She said to me, "I have your telegram with me." This telegram was one that I had sent to her mother [to give to the girl] when she was lying ill in hospital. She had so attracted the attention of

the nurses there, because no amount of morphia could stop the pain that she was suffering, and, when she had this telegram, she did not have a single moment's more pain until the time she passed into spirit…. This telegram she had had buried with her in the coffin, and she said she had it; she had still got it.

Witness: Margaret Lyons

Margaret Lyons had experiences and dialogue with her materialized father, showing he was alive although his body was dead. In his materialization he exhibited

- All his physical, mental, and memory characteristics, as he came very near to her and spoke with her
- His mental and sensory awareness when he remarked that Margaret was currently a very good teacher, although he had transitioned when she was only thirteen

Excerpts from the trial testimony follow.[17] You can listen to a narration of the testimony as you read it at www.afterlifeinstitute.org/margaret/.

Margaret Lyons: I recognized [my father] instantly by his face; his nose was broken and sort of went over a bit. When I heard Albert ask me to come forward, he said, "You are not afraid to come forward and see who this is?" When I saw him, I said, "Daddy." I was only thirteen when my daddy died, and I recognized him instantly. He said, "Marget." That was the name he called me "Marget," not "Margaret" and I stood sort of speechless. I could hardly believe the tremendous revelation. All he said to me was, "Yes, Marget, I am proud of you. You have made a far better teacher than ever I could make you." By those words he meant the fact that I wanted to be a schoolteacher, and him dying when I was only thirteen, the eldest of five of a family, I could not be a teacher, because my mother could not afford it, and it meant a good deal to me, those words. Nobody could fake those words; they were known only to me. He said, "I am proud of you, Marget. You are a better teacher than ever I could make you."...

I was asked by Albert, would I like to shake my father's hand; and I did. The hand was raised like that, and I took his hand. Then back to my mind came the small finger, with no bones; it was contracted. When I shook hands I said, "Your wee finger. It is really you." That is all....

He had very hard hands. That is one thing again that I noticed, his sort of horny hard hand, my daddy's hand, and my daddy's voice. No one could say my name as he did; I could never mistake that. He was of Irish parents. He had rather a way of saying it, which could not be said by anybody else.... I touched his face and felt the sort of bristly hair on his face as if unshaven. My daddy had a very short illness. He came home on the Wednesday from his work and died on the Monday morning. I remember that morning he died. His face had a sort of growth of hair which was pretty heavy, and that was one of the facts again that was noticeable when he appeared.

5. Montague Keen Materializes and Speaks to People Who Knew Him in This Life

Summary

Montague Keen materialized in a David Thompson séance and spoke to a group of sitters who knew him well.

Montague Keen

Montague Keen was a member of the Society for Psychical Research for fifty-five years. Principal investigator of the Scole Experimental Group, he died while giving a speech about the group at the Royal Society of Arts on January 15, 2004. During the next few months, he gave stunning evidence that he had survived the death of his body by coming through to mediums all over the world.

On April 16, 2004, five months after his transition, Monty, as they called him, spoke for twenty minutes to a group of sitters in a David Thompson séance, including Sandra and Robin Foy, founders of the Scole Experimental Group, and afterlife researcher Guy Lyon Playfair. Monty referred to the Enfield Poltergeist investigation that he had been involved in with Playfair, and gave the number of the house at the center of the investigation, which all involved had kept secret, evidence that it was Montague Keen who was speaking.

His materialization and addressing the sitters by name show he retained all his memories and mental faculties after his body had died. He referred to current events, showing he was alive contemporaneously. A portion of the séance follows. You can listen to this and the entire session in which he spoke at www.afterlifeinstitute.org/monty/.[18]

Transcript of an excerpt of the recording:

Monty: Hello.

Sitters: Hello.

Monty: Can you hear me?

Sitters: Yes, we can!

Monty: Am I speaking clearly?

Sitters: Yes, you are!

Monty: Oh, good. You know who it is, don't you?

Robin Foy: Monty.

Monty: Of course, it's Monty.

(laughter)

Monty: Are you here, Guy? (Guy Lyon Playfair, fellow researcher).

Guy: Yes, I'm over here.

Monty: Oh, good, good. I'm so glad that... that you're able to be here with the rest of them.

John Samson: Well. Me, too.

Monty: Yes, and... is that you, Sandra?

Sandra Foy: Yes, it is!

Monty: Oh, they [managed to get you here]

Sandra: Yes, they did. Yes.

Monty: [indistinct comment - fantastic?]

Sandra: It's wonderful to hear you, Monty.

Monty: Does my voice sound clear?

Sandra: It does. Very good. You've mastered it very well.

Evidence from Communication through Materialization Mediumship 57

Sitters: Yes. Very good.

Monty: Well. It... it's taken me a little bit of time.

Robin Foy: That's right, Monty. Yes.

Monty: There can be very little time... to, to, to... get it just right.

Sitters: Yes. Yes.

Monty: Now. It have a few things... that I... that I want to say

Sitters: Yes. OK.

Monty: to you all. First of all, to Guy.

Guy: Hmm.

Monty: It's not like Enfield, is it.

Guy: Not yet, no... but I'm sure you'll do your best.

Monty: You know what I'm talking about, don't you?

Guy: Indeed. Yes.

Monty: It's nothing like Enfield.

John: Well... I'm glad to hear that. [chuckle]

Monty: Do you know... I... I've investigated, since I've been over here, regarding Enfield, Greenstreet. I've investigated.

Monty: Can you hear me?

Guy: Yeah.

Monty: And I have to say that you was right in your assumptions that it was the young girl, Janet.

Guy: Hmm.

Monty:	It was her pituitary gland, coming into sexual awareness, puberty, that was creating the phenomena.
Guy:	Yes, it did coincide with her, her blood.
Monty:	Well. I can tell you that that's what it was.
John:	Hmm.
Monty:	And, and, and, Guy. I understand that you're going to talk at my... at my urm Day of Memory.
Guy:	Yes. Indeed.
Monty:	It seems so silly to say a Day of Memory...

(general laughter)

Monty:	when I'm still here, doesn't it!

Evidence from Materialization Mediumship Proves You Will Never Die

The individuals who materialized and spoke during these materialization-medium séances had all the qualities they had when living on earth: body structures, fluent voice, characteristic personality, memories of past events, and acknowledgement of current events. Their bodies died but they transitioned to the next stage of their lives where they continue to live, vibrant and happy. They were able to return to earth, take on the form of material bodies identical to those they had when on earth, converse with people who knew them well, and touch them, embrace them, and kiss them.

They carried on casual conversations as they did when they were on earth. The people in the séances accepted these conversations as valid because they recognized the person's unique body structure, voice quality, personality, references to current events, and reminiscences of past events in the people's lives.

These individuals who materialized during séances did not die when their bodies died. Evidence from the communication through materialization mediums proves you will never die.

Chapter 3

Communication through Instrumental Transcommunication Is Evidence You Will Never Die

Instrumental transcommunication (ITC) or electronic voice phenomena (EVP) uses technology to record voices or images of people now alive whose bodies have died. With the advent of recording technology, voices and images began to be recorded. The methods used were not systematized, and some worthwhile efforts were not continued by other researchers. However, in recent years new methods have emerged and are maturing.

EVP/ITC presents convincing evidence that consciousness survives the death of the body. As the discipline matures, the evidence will multiply. There are two reasons the audio and video recordings researchers are acquiring demonstrate that people whose bodies have died are living in the next realm of life:

1. The recordings are consistently a dialogue. People in spirit answer questions and make relevant responses. The respondents are clearly mentally functioning and have memories and knowledge only they could have.

2. The researchers ask to speak to specific people and those people respond with statements that identify them. They are actively engaged in the researchers' efforts. The speakers identify themselves as the people who have left the body behind and are now living in the next life.

EVP/ITC pioneers Friedrich Jürgenson and Konstantin Raudive recorded hundreds of voices with tape and digital recorders. Marcello Bacci and Anabela Cardoso have conversed with people living in spirit using "direct-radio voice." Other researchers have developed electronic devices, such as George Meek and Bill O'Neil's Spiricom and the sophisticated devices created by Hans Otto König.

But the most consistently successful methods that clearly record answers to questions posed by researchers and the family of the person in spirit are being developed by Sonia Rinaldi in Brazil and are being replicated by Sheri Perl in New York.

As ITC develops, the responses will become longer. Samples from the following researchers demonstrate that the people being questioned respond appropriately, showing they are alive.

1. Sonia Rinaldi's Instrumental Transcommunication

The most active, groundbreaking ITC researcher in the world today is Sonia Rinaldi of Brazil. Rinaldi creates new methods that continually improve voice and image recordings. The speakers converse with her and show awareness of what she is doing. She has done readings for as many as 163 parents in a month, recording as many as 200 messages in a session. Parents recognize the voices and images as their children, showing that the children are alive now, long after their bodies have died. She does her work for free.

Following are examples of Sonia's recordings that she has made available to parents of children who have transitioned from earth. You can listen to them at www.afterlifeinstitute.org/sonia/.

>**Sonia:** "Would you like to leave a message to your mother?"
>
>**Little girl:** "Mommy, I can talk."

Father: "I am sure you're doing great. We love you and miss you."

Kelsie: "Daddy, you know, love you."

Kelsie: "A miracle! Many for listening."

Kelsie: "Miss my daddy."

Sonia: "Jasmine, what you would like to say to your dad?"

Jasmine: "I love you."

Sonia: "Say something beautiful to your mother."

Jasmine: "Miss you."

Sonia: "What else you would like to say?"

Jasmine: "Don't cry."

Amber: "I didn't think it'd end."

Sonia: "This is love."

In this recording, Amber responds before her mother asks the question because she received her mother's thought before her mother asked it.

Amber: "I did work."

Mother: "Are you ready to work with Tesla and Sonia?"

Mother: "Sonia loves you and I love you."

Adam: "I love you, Mom."

Mother: "Hi, Brandon. How are you doing?"

Brandon: "Mommy, I'm following Grandpa."

Mother: "Hi Tyler. I love you, Baby."

Tyler: "Always. Life is crazy."

Tyler: "Mommy, I love you."

Mother: "I miss you."

Sonia: "Hi, Helen. How are you today?"

Helen: "Sounds very amazing."

At times the audio recordings match video recordings of transimages of the person communicating. When Sonia recorded my mother in preparation for a 2014 conference, she also recorded an image of her in spirit. The image she captured is on the left. On the right is a photograph of my mother in her twenties. It is a well-established fact that people on the next plane of life have the bodies they had in their twenties or thirties, the prime of their lives.

Sonia's Image of Craig's Mother (left) and Early Photograph (right)

In the audio recording of my mother, she answered the question before Sonia asked it. This is often the case because speakers from the next plane of life don't need the spoken words. They get the questions telepathically, so when Sonia thought of the question before asking it, my mother responded.

Craig's mother: "Ready at this point."

Sonia: "Can Mrs. Rosemary say something to Craig?"

The recording had the tone and quality of my mother's voice and the content I would expect from her. This recording is also at www.afterlifeinstitute.org/sonia/.

2. Sheri Perl's Instrumental Transcommunication

Sheri Perl is a researcher and minister to parents whose children have transitioned from the earth. She developed the Prayer Registry for the parents. At an Afterlife Research and Education Institute conference, Sheri learned Sonia's method and began using it to record voices of children in spirit to give to the parents.

These are examples of questions mothers have asked over the phone and their children's responses that Sheri recorded. You can listen to these at www.afterlifeinstitute.org/perl/.

Mother: "Hi, Sweety."

Son: "Hi, mom."

Mother: "Alexandria, are you happy?"

Child: "All the time."

Mother: "Are you in Heaven?"

Child: "I am."

Mother: "I love you, and I just want to know, do you still love me?"

Child: "I love you."

Mother: "Adam, it's Mom. I want to know, are you at peace?"

Child: "I am, Mommy."

Mother: "Hi, Justin, it's Mom."

Justin: "Hi, Mom."

Parents validate the recordings of their children, who are alive although their bodies have died. Example parent responses follow.

Parent 1 ~ "I have read the text and started listening—this is so, so very amazing!! It sounds just like Brent's voice in the one where he said that he was with my Dad—and this has been my deep feeling that he HAS been with my Dad, so that alone is such an affirmation. Then to hear Brent's voice saying the word "Dad"—how perfect!! My heart is singing and I want to listen to more and let you know if I hear Brent's voice again."

Parent 2 ~ So much of this is Ben and his dad... the references to Art and Arthur I think are my late husband but the Danny reference I think is referencing your son.... And the "Gerber" and "Doritos" messages, when Ben was young everyone said he looked like the Gerber baby and Ben's favorite snack was

Doritos....Truly amazing and so much validation... thank you, Sheri!

Parent 3 ~ This first EVP blew away all I expected ... took my breath away... no mistaking it... It seems it's not as clear to those who didn't know him ... but there is absolutely no mistaking his voice for me, his mother... I had to leave work and sit in my car and catch my breath and calm my heart ... Even though his answer was short it vibrated throughout my whole body to hear him. I feared his voice might sound different as you warned me sometimes it does... but this first EVP I heard was the voice I knew and loved for 27 years!!!! My question was... Justin, do you come visit me? And he replied in his earthly voice.... All the time... that is everything to me!!

Parent 4 ~ The best evidence I felt coming from my son through the EVP were 1) his voice was recognizable every time he said " I Love You." 2) He asked about his children, both of them. 3) He asked me if I was proud of him. He would always ask me that question when he was a child growing up. 4) As you know my son was a drug addict. He had seen me cry a lot and I would tell him I would do anything to get him off of heroin. He would always answer, "I am sorry, Mom." He said that so many times in his life and again on the EVP. 6) Because I was raising my grandchild (my son's kids) I had always felt guilty in many of my decisions to protect them from my own son's ravished drug use. Again he answered... "What you did, Mother, was the right thing." 7) I had a vision months after my son passed. It was of my son kneeling before a man in a white robe. My son also was in a white robe. My son was a Christian. I remember thinking to myself, "Has my son met Jesus?" In the EVP he clearly states "Jesus found me." Omg !! 8) Just about every morning between 3 and 4 a.m. I wake up wide awake. So awake that I just get up for the day. My son asks in the EVP if I would like to sleep in.... Yes yes yes I would, Brad. LOL. I still don't know why he wakes me up tho'. 9) I have had conversations with my son, either in my head or out loud. I always have gotten answers. But I second guess myself if it was really him. Once again in the EVP he answered... "I hear, Mom." So awesome."

Parent 5 ~ The first thing about the reading that made me positive you had gotten Luke is the multitude of comments he made. He always was hyper-verbal! So here's a list of my impressions:

When he said "I'm Luke"—that sounds like him.

Also, when he said "I love it here"—that sounds EXACTLY like him.

The numerous times he expressed his love for me is very much Luke. We told each other we loved each other all the time. Lots of hugs, too. :)

He said "I don't need money" followed by "thank you for offering." Luke used to ask me or my husband if he could have $4 (or some other low odd-ball amount of money) and we would always ask him if he needed more than that. He would always say, no thank you, but thanks for offering. Only my husband, Luke, and I would know what that means. It was extraordinary when I heard that.

He stated "We're off Ritalin." Luke was struggling with drug addiction when he died. I think that was his way of telling me they ALL are healed once they leave their bodies. It was reassuring and another way of him letting me know it was really him.

When I said goodbye to him, he responded "Goodbye, Mom, you're on my mind. I'll call you. You can feel that I come." He always said "I'll call you," always. And I think he was again reassuring me, with the "You can feel that I come." I CAN feel him when he's around. He was confirming that for me.

There is no doubt in my mind that the clips are Luke. Except for the one when I told our children I love them and the many voices answered 'We love you, too.' That one gives me wonderful chills. So much love.

3. Konstantin Raudive's Recorded Phone Calls from the Life after This Life to Well-Known Individuals

Dr. Konstantin Raudive was a Latvian writer, psychologist, and philosopher who studied psychotherapy under Carl Jung. He read a book by electronic voice phenomena (EVP) researcher Friedrich Jürgenson titled *Voices from Space* in which Jürgenson describes recording the voices of people whose bodies had been dead for years or decades. Raudive was determined to learn how to record such voices. He set up his equipment following Jürgenson's instructions. One night, he played back a recording he had made and heard distinct voices. He continued his effort and eventually had recorded over 72,000 EVP/ITC voice recordings. Based on his findings, he wrote *Breakthrough: An Amazing Experiment in Electronic Communication with the Dead*[19] published in 1971. Raudive transitioned from earth to the next stage of his life in 1974.[20]

In 1994, 20 years after his transition, he made phone calls to EVP/ITC researchers Sarah Estep, George Meek, Mark Macy, and Sonia Rinaldi. The phone calls to Sarah Estep and George Meek were recorded. Mark Macy was not available when Raudive called, but Raudive left him a recorded voice message. Sonia Rinaldi did not have a recorder on her phone. In the phone calls,

Raudive spoke articulately, referred to events in the listeners' lives, displayed his characteristic Latvian accent, and carried on a fluid dialogue about the work these researchers were doing in EVP/ITC. The conversations are evidence that Raudive continues to live although his body is dead.

Sarah Estep compiled the recordings and has made them available. You can hear her narration and Raudive's phone conversations at https://afterlifeinstitute.org/calls/.

4. George Meek and Bill O'Neil's Recorded Conversations with a Scientist in the Next Life

George W. Meek, director of Research Metascience Foundation, was a retired industrialist who had revolutionized the air-conditioning industry, resulting in a series of patents. At a séance attended by Meek, a spirit describing himself as "a discarnate scientist" gave Meek the idea of building a mechanical device that could be used to communicate with those living in the life after this life. Meek became obsessed with achieving such two-way conversation through an electronic device.

Six years later, Meek met a medium named Bill O'Neil who was an electronics engineer. O'Neil's spirit guide Doc Nick said he had been a ham radio operator during his life on earth and suggested using specific audio frequencies on the radio to record voices instead of the "white noise" used by most EVP/ITC researchers as background noise. Doc Nick gave O'Neil and Meek technical information for building the communications device and a list of frequencies for the background noise that might result in voice recordings.

Another person in spirit then joined the team. Dr. George Jeffries Mueller, a NASA scientist and physics professor who transitioned in 1967, materialized in O'Neil's living room at one of their sittings.

In October 1977, O'Neil and Meek built the first electronic device following the guidelines from Doc Nick. They named it Spiricom.[21] O'Neil and Meek began listening intently to the buzzing of the device that was a medium for the voices to come through. As they listened, Dr. Mueller spoke through the buzzing. To prove his identity, he gave his social security number, the place where his death certificate could be found, and intimate details of his life and scholastic achievements. He said he had been a NASA scientist and college professor before his body died in 1967. Meek and O'Neil checked out the information and all of it was correct.

The fact that Dr. Mueller was able to communicate with Meek and O'Neil ten years after his body had died demonstrates that he survived the death of his body. He was articulate, identified himself by name and position, and spoke about current occurrences.

You can view a video of O'Neil communicating with Dr. Mueller at https://afterlifeinstitute.org/spiricom/.

Evidence from Instrumental Transcommunication Proves You Will Never Die

The voices that ITC researchers are recording demonstrate that the people communicating are alive and articulate, although their bodies and brains have died. The people in spirit have all the qualities they had when living on earth: fluent voice, characteristic personality, memories of past events, and acknowledgement of current events. The people to whom the statements are addressed accept these conversations as valid because they recognize the person in spirit's voice quality, personality, references to current events, and reminiscences of past events in the people's lives.

These individuals who speak through ITC did not die when their bodies died. The evidence from these communications proves you will never die.

Chapter 4

Appearances by People after Their Bodily Deaths Are Evidence You Will Never Die

Many records exist of people whose bodies have died appearing and communicating with people living on the earth plane. They have all the body and voice characteristics of the deceased person, and they communicate with fluency about commonly held memories. Following are examples of spontaneous materializations from reliable sources.

1. Elisabeth Kübler-Ross Experiences a Materialization

Dr. Elisabeth Kübler-Ross was an internationally renowned physician, author, speaker, and expert on death and dying. She was one of *Time* magazine's hundred most important thinkers of the 20th century, and her 1997 book, *On Death and Dying,* was one of New York Public Library's Books of the Century. She received twenty honorary degrees for her achievements and published twenty books on death and dying. She was also included on the International Biographical Centre's list of the foremost women of the twentieth century.

Evidence That Dr. Kübler-Ross Saw and Conversed with Mrs. Schwartz, Whose Body Had Been Dead for Two Years

In her renowned 1991 book, *On Life After Death,* Dr. Kübler-Ross described a visitation in a physical form by someone who had passed away two years earlier. You can listen to a narration of this excerpt as you read it at www.afterlifeinstitute.org/kr/.

> I was at a crossroad. I felt I needed to give up my work with dying patients. That day, I was determined to give notice and leave the hospital and the University of Chicago. It wasn't an easy decision because I really loved my patients.
>
> I walked out of my last seminar on death and dying towards the elevator. At that moment, a woman walked towards me. She had an incredible smile on her face, like she knew every thought I had.
>
> She said, "Dr. Ross, I'm only going to take two minutes of your time. If you don't mind, I'll walk you down to your office." It was the longest walk I have ever taken in my life. One part of me knew this was Mrs. Schwartz, a patient of mine who had died and been buried almost a year ago. But I'm a scientist, and I don't believe in ghosts and spooks!
>
> I did the most incredible reality testing I've ever done. I tried to touch her because she looked kind of transparent in a waxy way. Not that you could see furniture behind her, but not quite real either. I know I touched her, and she had feeling to her.
>
> We came to my office, and she opened the door. We went inside, and she said, "I had to come back for two reasons. Number one, I wanted to thank you and Reverend Smith once more for what you have done for me. But the real

reason why I had to come back is to tell you not to give up your work on death and dying. Not yet."

I realized consciously that maybe indeed this was Mrs. Schwartz. But I thought nobody would ever believe me if I told this to anybody. They really would think I had flipped!

So my scientist in me very shrewdly looked at her and said, "You know, Reverend Smith would be thrilled if he would have a note from you. Would you terribly mind?" You understand that the scientist in me needed proof. I needed a sheet of paper with anything written in her handwriting, and hopefully, her signature.

This woman knew my thoughts and knew I had no intention to ever give her note to Reverend Smith. However, she took a piece of paper and wrote a message and signed it with her full name. Then, with the biggest smile of love and compassion and understanding, she said to me, "Are you satisfied now?"

Once more, she said, "You cannot give up your work on death and dying. Not yet. The time is not right. We will help you. You will know when the time is right. Do you promise?" The last thing I said to her was "I promise." And with that, she walked out.

No sooner was the door closed, I had to go and see if she was real. I opened the door, and there was not a soul in that long hallway![22]

Kübler-Ross was a highly respected psychiatrist who showed no sign of hallucinations and was mentally competent at the time of her experience. Kübler-Ross saw Mrs. Schwartz clearly as a physical body and touched her. Mrs. Schwartz referred to things that had happened to her and referred to events in Kübler-Ross's current life. She was articulate and showed no signs of defect from her body's death. The spontaneous materialization of Mrs. Schwartz, whose body had died two years before, is evidence that you will live on after your body dies.

2. Raymond A. Moody Experiences and Speaks with His Deceased Grandmother

Raymond A. Moody is a philosopher, psychologist, physician, and author. He is the author of *Life after Life*, which uses the term "near-death experience" for the first time. He is widely respected, of sound mind, and not given to hallucinations.

Evidence That Dr. Moody Saw and Spoke with His Grandmother

Dr. Moody had an experience in which his deceased grandmother materialized, had a lengthy conversation with him, and calmly left. His account of what happened follows. You can listen to a narration of the text at www.afterlifeinstitute.org/moody/.

> It is very difficult to put this experience into language; I am at a loss to explain some of it in words. Yet, I have no doubt whatsoever that I was in the presence of my deceased grandmother for an extended period and did in fact converse with her at length. At first, as I said, I did not recognize this person, though she immediately seemed somehow familiar. She looked somewhat as she had while alive on the earth, but appeared younger than she had been even when I was born. When I recognized her as my grandmother and confronted her with this fact, she immediately acknowledged it and began to use the nickname she alone had used for me when I was a child. She talked with me about events only my grandmother and I knew. She imparted to me certain very personal information about my early life that has been quite

important and revealing.... I might add that the relationship between me and my paternal grandmother had been rather difficult while she was alive. Yet, our meeting enabled us to smooth things over. I now see her humor and appreciate her as a person in a brand new way. I look forward to meeting her again when I make my transition.[23]

Later in the same essay, Dr. Moody explains that the experience he had with his grandmother had none of the characteristics of a hallucination.

I can attest that my own visit with my grandmother was radically different from anything I have experienced during my two decades of familiarity with hypnosis. As to "suggestion," the fact that some subjects in the study [described in this source document] saw someone other than the person they set out to see illustrates the difficulty in explaining these happenings solely in terms of that concept.[24]

Dr. Moody's grandmother materialized in a body he recognized as his grandmother. She was alive and articulate and had a fully functioning memory of events that had happened in the past, although her body and brain had been dead for years.

3. Rev. John Bertram Phillips Experiences a Materialization of C. S. Lewis

J. B. Phillips was an English Bible translator, author, and ordained Anglican priest responsible for the *Phillips Translation of the New Testament*. Phillips was an esteemed scholar with no history of hallucinations or mental illness. In these two incidents, the renowned author C. S. Lewis appeared to him before Phillips was aware Lewis had transitioned.

Evidence Demonstrating Phillips Conversed with C. S. Lewis

J. B. Phillips was suffering from a life-threatening depression. He refused to leave his room, would not eat, and would not exercise. He had begun to doubt God's love for him. His account of what happened from his book, *Ring of Truth*, follows. You can listen to a narration of the text at www.afterlifeinstitute.org/phillips/.

> Many of us who believe in what is technically known as the Communion of Saints must have experienced the sense of nearness, for a fairly short time, of those whom we love soon after they have died. This has certainly happened to me several times. But the late C. S. Lewis, whom I did not know very well, and had only seen in the flesh once, but with whom I had corresponded a fair amount, gave me an unusual experience. A few days after his death, while I was watching television, he "appeared" sitting in a chair within a few feet of me, and spoke a few words which were particularly relevant to the difficult circumstances through which I was passing. He was ruddier in complexion than ever, grinning all over his face and, as the old fashioned saying has it, positively glowing with health. The interesting thing to me was that I had not been thinking about him at all. I was neither alarmed nor surprised nor, to satisfy the Bishop of Woolwich, did I look up to see the hole in the ceiling that he might have made on arrival! He was just *there* —"large as life and twice as natural"! A week later, this time when I was in bed reading before going to sleep, he appeared again, even more rosily radiant than before, and repeated to me the same message, which was very important to me at the time. I was a little puzzled by this, and I mentioned it to a certain saintly Bishop who was then living in retirement here in Dorset. His reply was, "My dear J...., this sort of thing is happening all the time."[25]

Another source explains Phillips's reference to the "few words which were particularly relevant to the difficult circumstances through which I was passing."

In this vision, Lewis spoke only one sentence to Phillips: "J. B., it's not as hard as you think." One solitary sentence, the meaning of which is debated! But what is not debated is the effect of that sentence. It snapped Phillips out of his depression, and set him again following God. After Lewis spoke that cryptic sentence, he disappeared.

Phillips came out of his chambers only to find that Lewis had died moments before the appearance, miles away. He pondered this in his heart, with wonder, and never returned to his depression.[26]

Philips attested to the materialization of C. S. Lewis, but the most convincing evidence of its occurrence was the fact that it "snapped Phillips out of his depression and set him again following God." C. S. Lewis demonstrated that he was alive even though his body was dead.

4. People Appear to Loved Ones a Distance Away at the Moment of Their Transition

It is a common phenomenon for people whose bodies have just died to appear as a full, tangible body and converse with people who know them well hundreds or thousands of miles away from their dead bodies. Examples follow. In some cases, the person transitioning is seen by more than one person.

A man who was alone, reading, looked up from his book and clearly saw a school friend. The friend then disappeared. A day later he learned his friend's body had died at the same moment she had appeared to him.[27]

As a woman attending a family party climbed a set of stairs, a lady acquaintance passed her quickly. She wore black silk with a muslin covering over her head and shoulders. Her silk rustled. In a moment, she was gone. The woman was surprised because she did not know this acquaintance was at the party. The next morning a nursery girl who worked at the house was startled to see the same lady in black silk in a room. She refused to go into that room again. Shortly thereafter the woman learned that her acquaintance had passed away at the precise time she had seen her at the family party.[28]

An acquaintance of mine, Mike Thomson, described the unexpected appearance of his ex-wife's Uncle Neely. Mike hadn't seen his ex-wife's family since their divorce seven years before. One day, driving alone down a highway, he felt someone next to him. There in the passenger seat sat Uncle Neely. Mike was shaken because he was alone in the car. Uncle Neely said, "Mike, the Mass is over. Thanks be to God." That was an old joke Mike had had with him. Mike had converted to Catholicism for his wife but hated going to Mass. When the family attended mass together, Uncle Neely would smile at Mike as they walked out after mass and say, "Well, Mike, the Mass is over. Thanks be to God."

Mike looked again at the passenger seat. Uncle Neely was gone. When Mike arrived home he was upset and worried; he thought he might be losing his mind, so he didn't tell anyone about the strange event. About an hour later his son came into the room and said, "Dad, Mom called. She said she had some bad news. Uncle Neely died today." As Mike found out later, Uncle Neely had transitioned from his body at the moment he had appeared in Mike's car.

Other examples of such materializations at the moment of the transition follow.

Second Lieutenant Leslie Poynter was killed in action during World War I. At 9:00 one evening he appeared to his sister in England, walked into her bedroom, bent over, and kissed her. Smiling happily, he faded from view. Two weeks later, the family received a telegram informing them of his death on the date he had appeared to his sister.[29]

A woman named Mrs. Pacquet experienced her brother Edmund appearing to her mysteriously, although she knew he was at sea serving on a ship. He seemed to be acting out something. She later received word that, six hours before the appearance, he had drowned at sea. He was acting out how he had been caught around the legs by a rope and dragged overboard.[30]

A woman named Gladys Watson was awakened from a deep sleep by someone calling her name. As she awoke, she saw her paternal grandfather. He said to her, "Don't be frightened. It's only me. I've just died." She described what she had seen to her husband. He refused to believe her grandfather had visited her and telephoned the family home. He was surprised to learn that her grandfather had died unexpectedly that very evening.[31]

Lord Brougham, an English peer, was traveling in Sweden. He suddenly saw an apparition of a university friend he had not seen or thought about for years. Later he received a letter saying that the friend had died in India at the exact time he saw the apparition. The two had made a pact that whoever passed away first would appear to the other.[32]

Mrs. Arthur Bellamy made a similar agreement with a friend while at school. They had not seen each other for years, but a night after hearing of the friend's death Mrs. Bellamy's husband was startled to see a lady sitting on the bed beside his sleeping wife. He later saw a photograph of the school friend and said it was she whom he had seen.[33]

Dr. Minot J. Savage, a Unitarian clergyman, described an incident in which a young boy received a visit from a loving friend he called "Judge," who had just passed away. After the boy was put to bed one night, his parents heard him crying. They rushed to him and asked him what was wrong. Sobbing, he said, "Judge says he's dead! He has been here and told me that he is dead!" The next morning the parents learned that Judge had died at about that time the night before.[34]

Evidence from Appearances by People Whose Bodies Have Died Proves You Will Never Die

Many accounts exist of people appearing to loved ones or other people they know well years after their bodies have died or at the moment of their death. The witnesses are of sound mind, not given to hallucinations, often highly regarded for their achievements, and with no motive to create a fictitious account. The account can be by a naïve child who is shaken by the appearance. The people communicating are alive and articulate, although their bodies and brains have died. The people have all the qualities they had when living on earth: fluent voice, characteristic personality, memories of past events, and acknowledgement of current events. The people to whom the statements are addressed accept these conversations as valid because they recognize the person in spirit's appearance, voice quality, personality, references to current events, and reminiscences of past events in the people's lives.

The evidence from spontaneous appearances of people in spirit to individuals who knew them proves you will never die.

Chapter 5

Psychotherapist Afterlife Communication Experiences Are Evidence You Will Never Die

We would expect that if grieving people were able to communicate with loved ones living in the next life, psychotherapists would have developed ways to help them enter a state of mind in which they are able to do so. In fact, three successful methods have been developed and are used by psychotherapists today: Induced After-Death Communication, Repair & Reattachment Grief Therapy, and Loving Heart Connections. All three help grieving clients have their own afterlife communication experiences while sitting in their therapists' offices.

Participants insist they have had connections with their loved ones. Their grief reduces dramatically. At times they learn things they did not know that are later are confirmed.

1. Induced After-Death Communication Demonstrates That Consciousness Survives Bodily Death

In 1995 Dr. Allan Botkin, a psychotherapist at a Chicago VA hospital, was startled when one of his patients described having an after-death communication in his office. The procedure Dr. Botkin was using to help reduce the veteran's grief was eye movement desensitization and reprocessing (EMDR). In EMDR the psychotherapist has patients move their eyes back and forth rapidly as they would in REM (rapid eye movement) sleep. The procedure is called "bilateral stimulation" because it results in alternating stimulation of either side of the body. In the case of eye movements, alternating stimulation is of the right and left visual cortexes. Other stimulation of either side of the body is made using tapping, vibrations, and varying tones or music volume alternating between ears.

After a set of these stimulations, the patients close their eyes and usually experience profound breakthroughs in understanding. No one is quite sure how it works, but it has proved to be one of the most powerful therapeutic tools the discipline of psychology has ever discovered. To date over 10,000 psychotherapists have been trained to use it and it has been endorsed by many psychological and health organizations, including the American Psychological Association and Veterans Health Administration.

The Vietnam combat veteran Dr. Botkin was working with had been experiencing devastating grief for decades from intrusive memories of a young Vietnamese orphan he had come to love as a daughter, but who died in his arms from a bullet wound. During an EMDR session, the vet said that while his eyes were closed he saw the girl as a beautiful young woman, not the child he had known. That matches mediums' descriptions of what happens when children die—they grow up in the life after this life. The vet's experience healed his grief instantly, and he was certain the girl was alive in the life after this life.[35]

Over the next few weeks 15 percent of Dr. Botkin's patients experienced similar after-death communications with people for whom they were grieving. He named the experience an induced after-death communication (IADC).[36]

In the ensuing months Dr. Botkin learned how to use IADC intentionally and had a high success rate with grieving veterans. He has since trained hundreds of psychotherapists to administer the therapy; thousands have now had an IADC experience. In virtually every case it alleviates grief almost immediately. Most patients emphatically state that they have had a real communication with their deceased loved ones, and even those who started the therapy as atheists view the life after this life differently.

As evidence of the validity of IADC, in many sessions patients have learned things they weren't expecting to learn and couldn't have known. The source must have been the deceased. For more about the method and therapist contact information visit www.induced-adc.com. Watch videos of people who have had the procedure at www.earthschoolanswers.com/iadc/.

The book I co-authored with Dr. Botkin, *Induced After-Death Communication: A New Therapy for Grief and Trauma*, describes eighty-four IADC cases.[37] Five of these follow. In all cases, the patients had sets of the bilateral stimulation and then sat quietly with eyes closed. The IADC unfolded naturally without prompting from Dr. Botkin. He didn't learn about the experiences until the patients opened their eyes and described them.

In the first case, a reporter had a session with Dr. Botkin as part of her interview of him. She reported having an IADC in which she experienced a deceased friend playing with a dog. The friend told the reporter that the dog was his sister's, although the reporter didn't know the woman had a dog. After the session, she called the woman and asked her. She replied, "Yes, I had a dog, but he died." She then described the dog, which was the same breed and color as the one the reporter had seen in the IADC.

The reporter also received a message for Dr. Botkin. The reporter looked exactly like an old friend the doctor had known years before, and he kept having flashbacks of his friend during the session. At one point during the IADC, the reporter told Dr. Botkin that her deceased friend said, "That was a long time ago, Dr. Lil," although she didn't understand what it meant. But Dr. Botkin knew immediately. His patients called him "Dr. Al," which was what the reporter was actually hearing. His deceased friend knew what Dr. Botkin was thinking about the reporter's resemblance to her.[38]

In the second evidentiary case, a patient's deceased father told him, "Forgive me for being so cold when we adopted you." That made no sense to the man because he remembered his father as always warm and close to him. That evening he asked his mother, "Was Dad cold to me when I was young?" His mother gasped and said, "Yes. How could you have remembered that? You were only a tiny baby." She explained that his father had been cold to him when he was an infant and wouldn't hold him, but after a few months everything was fine, and the patient grew up to have a very close relationship with his father. He had learned something in the IADC he couldn't have learned from any source other than his deceased father.[39]

In the third case, a blue-eyed Swedish veteran sought to have an IADC with a black soldier in his Vietnam platoon who died in a firefight. He told Dr. Botkin that there had been racial tension in the platoon, and that he was experiencing grief over the death. After the inducing procedure, when the patient opened his eyes, he looked perplexed. "The guy saw right through me," he said. He explained that he had only wanted to find out the soldier's name for paperwork that would get him additional money for the grief he claimed to suffer. The VA gave money monthly to vets who could prove they had some trauma that was causing them grief. But when the vet asked for the soldier's name in the IADC, the soldier said, "Why do you want my name now? You didn't want it then." The vet muttered again, "The guy saw right through me," and never raised the issue again in therapy.[40]

The deceased black soldier told the patient something he was not expecting. It could only have come from a living person who was not willing to cooperate with the subterfuge.

In the fourth case a Vietnam veteran wanted to reduce his consuming anger, which had lasted thirty-one years, with his commanding officer for sending him into combat without a rifle. Dr. Botkin couldn't use IADC to communicate with a living person, so he used EMDR to work on the anger. But when the man closed his eyes after his eye movements, he was surprised to see the commanding officer standing before him. The officer said he was very sorry for what he had done and realized the problems it caused the vet in his life. "He looked like he really meant it," the vet said. "I believe him." The anger resolved itself after all those years. Dr. Botkin was surprised that a living person had come through in an IADC session. But the next day the vet checked the lists of everyone who had died in the war and discovered that his commanding officer had died soon after the vet left Vietnam.[41]

The final example is a touching story of a man named Jim who had an IADC to resolve the grief over the death of his friend, Simon. You can listen to a narration of the text of this account at www.afterlifeinstitute.org/jim/.

Jim had been very close to Simon and his wife, Darlene. In the IADC Jim saw Simon and talked with him. Afterward he opened his eyes and told Dr. Botkin, "I feel he's OK. But you know, I was really hoping to have a message for Darlene. She's not doing well at all." Dr. Botkin induced another communication so Jim could ask for the message, but this time he only saw two hands—a broad, masculine hand over a feminine hand—which he felt were Simon's and Darlene's. Although he was elated by the contact with his friend, he was disappointed that he still had no message for Darlene.

After the session Jim went to Darlene's home. He told her he had communicated with Simon but was disappointed that he hadn't received a message for her, that he had only seen Simon's hand on top of hers. She began to cry, smiling and nodding, and said, "Last night I had a dream. It was so clear, it didn't seem like a dream. I felt, really felt, Simon holding my hand. Jim, he did give you a message from him to me. He was saying that it really was him holding my hand last night."[42]

These experiences are connections with the living person who has never gone far and is just not using a body anymore. IADCs occur when the psychotherapist helps patients set aside anger, guilt, shame, and other negative emotions using powerful EMDR therapy. That leaves only deep, underlying sadness. The psychotherapist then takes patients into that sadness, plumbing its depths without flinching from it, until they experience the most painful reaches of it. The patients, most often in tears, then closes their eyes and remain open to whatever will happen.

When all negative emotions and the deep sadness are out of the way, what is left is the compassion and love that created the sadness. That compassion and love drops the veil between the earth plane and the life after this life, and the IADC occurs. Then the loved one, who has always been alive, well, loving, and caring, is able to communicate. The results are rich, inspiring, loving reunions that heal grief. Those we love and feel compassion for are never far from us. We just can't quiet the noise of the earth plane to communicate with them. The IADC psychotherapy method does that.

2. Repair & Reattachment Grief Therapy Helps People Have Afterlife Communication

Repair & Reattachment Grief Therapy, developed by Rochelle Wright, a Washington state-licensed psychotherapist, reduces or virtually eliminates the deep grief in which a person is immersed. In a session, the therapist helps a client whose loved one is now living in the life after this life personally connect with the loved one. No medium is involved. The messages come directly to the person while they sit with their eyes closed.

Wright improved on Dr. Botkin's procedure by adapting EMDR to the unique requirements of communicating with someone living in the next life. The communication unfolds naturally when a facilitator helps the person enter a state in which the connection occurs, guided by those on the next plane of life. The facilitator does not lead or prompt the person. The procedure is 98 percent successful and, in a single session, reduces patient estimates of their grief from ratings of 10 or higher on a 10-point scale of disturbance to scores of 0 to 3.[43]

The procedure reorients the beliefs, images, feelings of guilt and anger, trauma, and perspectives on the loved one's passing so they are replaced by reassurance, joy, a renewed feeling of love and connection, and peace. The sadness at this separation through the passing is usually desensitized so the person doesn't remember it in the same way, so the sadness dissipates.

Thousands of sessions have now been performed. Many patients validate that connections are with people living in the next life.

In one example, Carole connected with her daughter, Kate, who had been killed in a car accident. During the session she received a validation of the experience from her friend Linda's son, Martine, who also was in spirit. You can hear Carole describing her afterlife connection at www.earthschoolanswers.com/carole/.

> After another set of eye movements, Carole closed her eyes again. "Now I see Martine, Linda's son. He passed away eight months ago. He's sitting on his couch looking at me,

with one leg up and his arms dangling in a funny pose, smiling. But I can still see Kate. Martine's flashing in and out. Now there are two things going on. Kate's outside and Martine's inside. He has his leg up with his arms in that funny position. I can see Kate's dress, but not the bottom. It keeps going to Martine sitting on the couch being silly. I don't understand this."

After the session, Carole wrote [Rochelle] an email describing a remarkable validation of her afterlife connection. She wrote that as she and Linda, Martine's mother, were riding home, she told Linda that she had seen Martine in her guided afterlife connection. Carole showed Linda the comical pose he was in, with his leg up and arms dangling. Linda's eyes opened wide. She said when Martine was clowning around he would make what they called his "monkey pose," with his leg up and arms dangling. It was exactly what Carole saw, without knowing that Martine did that.

The pose was a distinctive message from Martine to let his mom, Linda, know that he was fine, happy, and clowning as he always did. [44]

You can read more about the procedure in the book I co-authored with Rochelle, *Repair & Reattachment Grief Counseling.* You can watch videos of people describing their afterlife communication experiences at www.earthschoolanswers.com/rochelle/.

3. Loving Heart Connections Have Been Shown to Help People Communicate with Loved Ones

Ohio State-licensed psychotherapist Dr. Jane Bissler developed an afterlife communication method called Loving

Heart Connections in which people contact a psychotherapist online.[45] Sessions are private, use free online video-conferencing, and last about 90 minutes. Afterward the therapist teaches patients how to use the method on their own to continue having connections.

The method builds on scientific research and psychotherapies that provide a channel through which afterlife communication can be directly experienced. The two other methods therapists use are based on the same principles as Loving Heart Connections.

In the first test of this protocol, seventeen of eighteen participants had successful personal connections that they testified were very real and heartfelt to them.

A woman had a Loving Hearts Connection session in which she communicated with her son who transitioned at age twelve. She had the experience on her own with her eyes closed, then explained it to the psychotherapist. The following appears with her gracious permission. You can listen to a narration of the text at www.afterlifeinstitute.org/lhc/.

> There was a light. I think William appeared shortly after that. He looked so good. He was wearing a yellow Adidas t-shirt. Then William showed me this big pink flower, and it was so weird it was like the flower was alive. It was so fresh and moist. It was like the flower could breathe. There was a lake and lily pads with more flowers and William said, "Lotus Land." He said the flower was a lotus. I never would have known this. Then off a bit to the left there was this amazing show of colors; it was Aurora Borealis. It was not like the Aurora Borealis we have here in Alberta. This was like Aurora Borealis cranked up like you have never seen! It was mind blowing and magical. The colors were like I could go in the colors.

William said he liked where he was. He missed and loved me. He asked if I could come there. He said there is every kind of ice cream there that you can imagine, even cherry chunks in vanilla which was his favorite. He said our dog Hershey cannot yet see him in spirit.

Then he took me down a road. It was like I was with him. I could see every pebble. He took me to an old covered wagon. There was a man sitting on the little wagon bench. He was older, had grey hair and a beard and was wearing one of those hats like they wear in the Australian outback. He was slim and had on a white shirt and brown pants with suspenders. He did not say anything to me or acknowledge me. The wagon I could see in such detail that I could see where the cloth of the covered part attached to the wagon part. I could see some loose threads. The wagon was being pulled by two enormous beautiful black Clydesdale horses. They were magnificent. I looked directly into their eyes and they looked back at me like they were an inch from my face. I could feel their breath and the softness of their nostrils. They had white fur on their legs down near their hooves. I could see the fur so clearly like little bits of dirt in the fur. It was so clear. I cannot describe how clear this was it was just so amazing.

I think at this point I had almost forgot I was sitting in a chair. I was so engrossed in my surroundings. William said he liked riding in the back of the wagon. Then at that point I could feel William was leaving. He said he would see me later and he loved me.[46]

You can learn more at www.clearingyoursoul.com/loving-heart-connections/.

Evidence from Psychotherapist Connections Proves You Will Never Die

A primary role of the psychotherapist is to help people understand reality. They do not encourage or precipitate fantasy or illusion. The fact that people in grief are experiencing what they insist are communications with loved ones during a session with a qualified psychotherapist is evidence that the people communicating from the life after this life are alive even though their bodies have died. The results verify this reality—in a single session participants' grief reduces from ratings of 10 and "10 plus plus plus" on the 10-point Subjective Units of Disturbance (SUDS) self-rating scale to ratings of 0 to 3. The experiencers are profoundly moved and learn things they could not have known that prove true.

Successful, life-changing communications clients have with loved ones whose bodies have died that are facilitated by qualified psychotherapists is more evidence that proves you will never die.

Chapter 6

Self-Guided Afterlife Connections Are Evidence You Will Never Die

After I co-authored the books on Induced After-Death Communications and Repair & Reattachment Grief Therapy with the originators of those methods, I realized that people could have their own afterlife connections if they knew how to enter the relaxed state facilitated by psychotherapists. So I developed the Self-Guided Afterlife Connections Procedure for the Afterlife Research and Education Institute to allow people to have their own afterlife connections without the aid of a facilitator, medium, or therapist. It is free and available online at www.earthschoolanswers.com/selfguided/. Thousands of people have now gone through the training.

In the Self-Guided Afterlife Connections Procedure, the individual goes through eight stages of training in how to self-hypnotize. The first two stages explain the need for confidence that the afterlife is a reality and that their loved ones are available to communicate. The third takes them into a hypnotic state through a guided meditation. In this stage, participants learn to allow unfoldments to occur in their minds without trying to inhibit them or manipulate what happens. The next four stages guide increasingly independent self-inductions. After the last stage, the participant is able to perform self-hypnosis and have a connection with a loved one in the life after this life at any time, without aids such as a narration or music.

The result is that 86 percent of participants who complete the training confirm having successful connections, which contain many validations that participants are communicating with loved ones.

Example 1

A woman had already connected with her mother when the scene changed. You can listen to a narration of this text at www.afterlifeinstitute.org/selfguided1/.

> Then, I saw a young girl/teenager. She had familiar features. The name Brenda came to me and I realized it's a friend of mine's daughter. She died in a rollover crash where she was pinned and asphyxiated. The kids with her were allegedly responsible for her being abandoned at the wreck. The feelings I got from her had nothing to do with that wreck or the people around her then. She hovered with me, morphing a bit so I saw her in different stages, ages. I saw her exploring. I saw her as a student, studying. I don't know that she did that on Earth but she is now that she's passed. I heard her say, "I love mom. I miss mom." I asked in my mind, "How can you miss her, you are always with her?" It was more like a misunderstanding. I saw some food item, rolled. It looked like a lobster roll but with jalapeños. I was focused on it too much and it disappeared. I looked to the side and saw her as a little girl, rolling out dough, working on a red checked tablecloth, working so hard. She was darling! Then, I realized, Oh, she misses doing this stuff with her mom. At least that's what I got from it. I saw her enjoying the weather, the fall, the leaves, colors. I saw her and felt her loving the ocean and tide. I could

feel her sort of drinking it in. She showed me some other things she was liking about where she was and her condition.

IN AN EMAIL SHE SENT LATER, SHE WROTE,

Well, how Dee doo? I wrote Lauren [mother of Brenda in the afterlife connection] and told her the first part of it and how confused I was with the roll ups that had jalapeño in them. I kept thinking, "What on earth!?" So, I wrote Lauren unsure of how much to tell her. I can never remember who is a believer and who isn't. Guess what? She writes back and says it makes sense to her. Yes, they made jalapeño roll ups. WHAT.... I've NEVER heard of such a thing. Look, if I ever thought I was making this stuff up, well, I completely believe now. Where the hell did jalapeño rollups come from?

Example 2

You can listen to a narration of this text at www.afterlifeinstitute.org/selfguided2/.

I went to the same garden (my own) and again found what I did not expect. My Uncle Jim (who died about the same time as my father) was sitting in the seat my brother Dick had been in. Bob was my favorite uncle when I grew up. He used to take me for rides in his truck when he was working. I have not thought of him for some time. He began talking to me about the farm where I grew up. We walked out from the farmhouse and he began sharing about how it was when he grew up there. I had not thought of that much; both he and my Dad spent their childhood there. I turned to look at the ridge where I used to walk and daydream. Immediately he took both of us to the ridge. He said it was one of his favorite places too. Then he talked about how they dug out the white chalk rock there to make my Grandma's flower beds. It was a revelation to me: I had always loved the raised round flower beds in the front yard and I always loved the broken up place on the ridge but I had never put two and two together. Then Bob took me up high to look down on the farm. He asked me if I would like to take care of a farm for my remaining years. I said I was a bit old to do that. He waited for me to answer. I said "Sure." It seemed and still seems a strange idea. We left it there, said goodbye and separated.

Not what I expected. Just a chatty visit with someone I had not seen for some time. Different members of my family have been showing up. We were never an overtly affectionate bunch. All three sessions have seemed to convey a rather amused and affectionate attitude towards me. I have felt very much at home with them, always felt surprised at what transpires and left wondering at them in a good way.

Evidence from Self-Guided Connections Proves You Will Never Die

People's ability to initiate communications with their loved ones shows that the loved ones are still alive, just in a different form. They become present when asked, communicate information the experiencer would not have imagined, and reveal facts the experiencers knew nothing about but were later confirmed. The result is a dramatic reduction in grief and a desire to engage in more communications. The experiencers insist they have had a valid, uplifting communication with their loved one living in the life after this life.

Self-Guided Afterlife Connections are more evidence that proves you will never die.

Chapter 7

Communication through Trance Mediumship Is Evidence You Will Never Die

Trance mediums enter a state of trance during which people living in the life after this life use the mediums' bodies and vocal mechanisms to move and speak to sitters. The entities coat the mediums' vocal cords or create a separate vocal mechanism in the mediums' throat to fit the voice characteristics of the person in spirit. The mannerisms, voice, and content of the messages are not those of the medium.

We might wonder when the voices and content are coming from those in spirit or whether they are being fabricated, perhaps unconsciously, by the medium. There are two reasons we know the communications are coming from the person in spirit:

- Studies of brain-wave patterns show different entities are taking over the medium's mind.
- The contents of the messages have detail not known to the medium that could come only from the person in spirit.

Explanations of these reasons we know the communications are coming from the person in spirit follow.

Studies Show Different Entities Are Taking Over the Medium

To test the validity of trance mediums, history professor Charles Hapgood tested medium Elwood Babbitt using an electroencephalograph (EEG). He measured changes in brain-wave patterns when Babbitt was not in a trance and when he was taken over by people in spirit during trances. If the EEG patterns were the same, it would indicate that Babbitt could be consciously or subconsciously creating the voices. Hapgood recorded Babbitt's EEGs while three different entities were in control of him. The EEGs were found to be completely different from each other and from Babbitt's own EEG. An expert who interpreted the EEGs stated that they were characteristic of four people of different physical ages and could not belong to one person.[47]

The Message Content Could Come Only from the Person in Spirit

In each of the examples that follow, the information coming from the person in spirit is highly specific and could not be known by the medium. There are comments about current events, information inaccessible to the medium's mind that is validated, and technical details the mediums could not know. The messages are characteristic of the person in spirit.

1. Rev. Charles Drayton Thomas Communicates with His Father through Medium Gladys Osborne Leonard

Summary

Trance medium Gladys Osborne Leonard received messages from Rev. Charles Drayton Thomas's father referring him to text in specific parts of books and newspapers. The accuracy of his messages demonstrated that the elder Thomas was alive in spirit, communicating to his son about current activities.

Gladys Osborne Leonard

When Gladys Osborne Leonard entered hypnotic trances, she was taken over by a "control" personality named "Feda," who spoke in a childlike, lisping, high-pitched tone. Occasionally, the individuals in spirit would speak directly through Leonard.

For over forty years Mrs. Leonard's mediumship was studied exhaustively by members of the Society for Psychical Research. She was able to satisfy every test she was subjected to, and the researchers were convinced Mrs. Leonard was indeed speaking with living individuals who were simply no longer using a body.

Rev. Charles Drayton Thomas

The Rev. Charles Drayton Thomas, a Wesleyan minister and member of the British Society for Psychical Research (SPR), sat with Mrs. Leonard over one hundred times to test her abilities.

Evidence Demonstrating People Transition but Do Not Die

Thomas's deceased father instructed him, through Mrs. Leonard, to go to the lowest shelf in his extensive library and extract the sixth book from the left. On page 149, three-quarters of the way down, he was told, he would find a word that meant "falling back or stumbling." Once home, Thomas located the book and on page 149, three-quarters of the way down, were these words: "... to whom a crucified Messiah was an insuperable stumbling-block."

In eighteen months of experiments, Thomas's father was able to cite ever more words and numbers with increasing accuracy, both in Thomas's library and in a friend's. All were accurate.

Thomas decided to try asking his father for information from newspapers and magazines not yet printed. On January 16, 1920, Thomas's father in spirit told him to examine the *Daily Telegraph* the following day and to notice, near the top of the second column of the first page, the name of the place Thomas was born, Victoria Terrace on Victoria Street, Taunton. When Thomas checked the paper the next day, the word "Victoria" was in that exact spot, demonstrating that his father was alive contemporaneously and capable of researching the text and conveying it through the medium.

2. George Pelham Communicates with Richard Hodgson through Medium Leonora Piper

Summary

George Pelham, a lawyer, died in an accidental fall at age thirty-two. Five weeks later, Pelham's good friend John Hart attended a séance with trance medium Leonora Piper, who announced that Pelham was there to speak. Pelham provided a long list of details about himself, his early life, his friends, and his family. All were verified, demonstrating that Pelham was alive, with a fully intact memory and ability to converse long after his body had died.

Leonora Piper

Leonora Piper was a nineteenth-century trance medium who allowed communicators to speak through her vocal organs or through automatic writing. Piper was tested repeatedly by a wide range of skeptical observers. The Society for Psychical Research conducted several thousand sittings over two decades with carefully controlled environments to preclude fraud. The messages during the sittings were remarkably accurate. The unmistakable content and detail convinced the sitters their loved ones had spoken using Piper's vocal mechanism.

Dr. James Hyslop, a professor of logic and ethics at Columbia University and initially a skeptic, accepted the reality of the life after this life as a result of his studies of Piper, who repeatedly produced high-quality evidence. He concluded,

> I regard the existence of discarnate spirits as scientifically proved and I no longer refer to the skeptic as having any right to speak on the subject. Any man who does not accept the existence of discarnate spirits and the proof of it is either ignorant or a moral coward. I give him short shrift, and do not propose any longer to argue with him on the supposition that he knows anything about the subject.[48]

Richard Hodgson

Richard Hodgson was a researcher into mediumship in the nineteenth century who was a leading member of the Society of Psychical Research and the American Society for Psychical Research. Hodgson had a Doctor of Law degree. Joseph McCabe, an English writer called "one of the great mouthpieces of freethought in England"[49] praised Hodgson's work in debunking fraudulent mediums. He studied extensively the mediumship of the Italian medium Eusapia Palladino and Piper. The source of the account described here is an article in the *Proceedings of the Society for Psychical Research*.[50]

Evidence Demonstrating People Transition but Do Not Die

George Pelham, a lawyer and acquaintance of Hodgson, followed Hodgson's work with Leonora Piper and was skeptical about life after this life, calling it inconceivable. Nevertheless, he told Hodgson that if he died he would try to contact him. At age thirty-two, Pelham died in an accidental fall. Five weeks later Piper sat in a séance with Hodgson and John Hart, Pelham's close friend. She announced that Pelham was there to speak.

Pelham's spirit provided a long list of details about himself, his early life, his friends, and his family that could be verified to prove he was indeed George Pelham, still alive in the life after this life. All the details were verified as being true. For example, at the séance John Hart wore the shirt studs Pelham's father had given him as a memento after his friend's death. Pelham identified the studs as formerly his and explained how his mother had chosen them and his father had delivered them to Hart.[51]

In a different sitting, Pelham told Hodgson he had seen his father take a photograph of him to an artist to have it copied. After the séance Hodgson contacted Pelham's mother, who verified that, in fact, her husband had taken a photograph of their son to an artist to be copied.

> Pelham's father eventually wrote to Hodgson, "The letters you have written to my wife giving such extraordinary evidence of the intelligence exercised by George in some incomprehensible manner over the actions of his friends on earth have given food for constant reflection and wonder. (My) preconceived notions about the future state have received a severe shock."[52]

The details provided by Pelham in spirit were of details unknown to the medium that occurred after his body had died.

3. Richard Hodgson Communicates with a Good Friend after His Friend's Bodily Death

Summary

Hodgson had made a pact with his good friend George Pellow that whoever transitioned first would communicate with the other if communication were possible. Pellow was the first to transition from this life. Hodgson set up circumstances in which to test the mediumship of Leonora Piper while attempting to communicate with his friend in spirit.

George Pellow

George Pellow was an academic who was the author of *Jane Austen's Novels*, the first dissertation written about Austin's work. Pellow died at the age thirty-two in mysterious circumstances.

Evidence Demonstrating People Transition but Do Not Die

Over several months Hodgson introduced over 150 sitters at séances to the entranced Piper. Thirty of these had known Pellew while he was alive; the others had never met him. Pellew was able to correctly identify all the sitters he had known. Most of them talked and reminisced with Pellew, speaking through Piper as if he himself were there in the flesh. These meetings were so impressive that Hodgson wrote in his report that he was wrong in his earlier reports and that now he had irretrievably accepted the existence of the afterlife. He claimed that he had communicated with intelligences from the afterlife, and he couldn't wait to get there himself![53]

These communications demonstrated that Pellew was alive, with his personality, memories, and mental capacities intact.

4. Family Members Verified Communication with Their Daughter Whose Body Had Died

Rev. and Mrs. S.W. Sutton

In another sitting Piper was asked by the Rev. and Mrs. S.W. Sutton if she could communicate with their deceased little girl, Katherine, whose body had died six weeks before.

Evidence Demonstrating People Transition but Do Not Die

The account of the séance is now in the archives of the Society for Psychical Research.

Piper was able to establish contact between the Suttons and their very much-loved little girl from the afterlife. The information left no doubt whatsoever that the little girl was actually communicating from the afterlife with her mother and father still living on the earth plane.

She confirmed that she used to bite buttons. She identified her Uncle Frank and a friend who had died with a tumor and made reference to her brother by his pet name. She made reference to her sore throat and paralyzed tongue and that her head used to get hot before her death. She referred to Dinah her doll, to her sister Maggie, and to her little toy horse. She also sang two songs, the same songs she had sung immediately before she died. The Suttons had no doubt that they had made contact with their little girl and were especially happy when she reassured them: "I am happy... cry for me no more."[54]

Their daughter's accurate communication demonstrated she was alive after her body had died.

5. Flight Lieutenant H. C. Irwin Communicates to the British Air Ministry through Medium Eileen Garrett

Summary

Medium Eileen Garrett held a séance on October 7, 1939, during which a flight lieutenant killed in an airship crash came through. The officer described the airship's destruction in great detail. The account was presented to Air Ministry Intelligence, who were impressed by the accuracy and by details they had not known. Representatives of the ministry met with Garrett and interviewed the officer through her, discovering important, technical information Garrett could not have known. The accounts that follow are taken from psychical researcher Harry Price's records.[55]

Eileen Garrett

Eileen J. Garrett was a twentieth-century psychic and trance medium. From 1932 to 1933 she toured the United States, holding sittings with a number of organizations, including Johns Hopkins University and the New York Psychiatric Institute. She was actively involved in experimentation and study of the fundamentals of mediumship and psychic activity to evaluate and understand the actions and processes involved.

Flight Lieutenant Herbert Carmichael "Bird" Irwin

Flight Lieutenant Herbert Carmichael Irwin commanded non-rigid airships during World War I. He and forty-five other crew members were killed when Airship R101 crashed in a storm in Northern France on a flight from Britain to India.[56]

Evidence Demonstrating People Transition but Do Not Die

One of Garret's séances was interrupted by a man who identified himself as Flight Lieutenant H. C. Irwin of Airship R101. The sitters later learned that the airship had crashed three days before, but the government had not revealed the tragedy.

Irwin described the crash in detail, and one of the sitters chronicled his narrative in shorthand. The notes were presented to Air Ministry Intelligence, who were startled and impressed by the accuracy as well as by details they had not known. They were sufficiently convinced of the authenticity that Major Oliver Villiers arranged seven more séances with Garrett to hear more details from Irwin. He discussed technical subjects Garrett could not have understood, such as "useful lift of the airship," "gross lift," "disposable lift," "fuel injection," "cruising speed," "trim," "volume of structure," and others.

Irwin also discussed a top-secret, classified experiment the ministry had been engaged in: attempts to use a mixture of hydrogen and oil in airships. Ministry officials agreed that the information that came from Irwin through Garrett was completely accurate, even the town the airship passed over before it crashed and the locations of hidden diaries crew members had kept that revealed their fears about the secret project.[57]

Garrett's lack of technical knowledge, and an account so accurate that Air Ministry Intelligence arranged to interview Irwin through her, demonstrate that Flight Lieutenant Irwin was alive, had intact memories, and was articulate and capable of explaining technical information clearly.

6. Raymond Lodge Communicates through Two Trance Mediums

Summary

Through mediums, Raymond Lodge communicated many messages to his father, Sir Oliver Lodge, including information about his life that only intimate family members would know.

Sir Oliver Lodge

Sir Oliver Lodge was a British physicist who described electromagnetic radiation and held key patents for radio devices.

Raymond Lodge

Raymond Lodge was the youngest surviving son of Sir Oliver. Raymond Lodge became an electrical and mechanical engineer and worked in his brothers' business. In September 1914 Raymond volunteered for World War I military service and was a Second Lieutenant in the South Lancashire Fusiliers. He was killed in action in September 1915 at the age of twenty-six.

Evidence Demonstrating People Transition but Do Not Die

Through mediums, Raymond communicated many messages to his father, including information about his life that only intimate family members would know. Sir Oliver stated absolutely that they showed beyond reasonable doubt he and his family were receiving communications from Raymond.[58]

On September 27, 1915, at a séance with materialization medium A. Vout Peters, attended by an anonymous person known only as M. F. A. L., Peters' control "Moonstone" spoke through Peters:

> You have several portraits of this boy [Raymond]. Before he went away you had got a good portrait of him—two—no, three. Two where he is alone and one where he is in a group of other men. He is particular that I should tell you of this. In one you see his walking-stick—("Moonstone" here put an imaginary stick under his arm).[59]

Upon reading M. F. A. L.'s account of the séance, Sir Oliver said he had single photographs of Raymond, but no group photo.

On November 29 Mrs. Lodge received a letter from the mother of a captain who had known Raymond. She wrote about the nature of Raymond's fatal wound and said she had a photo of a group of officers, including Raymond, taken in August. She offered to send a copy.[60]

On December 3 Sir Oliver was a sitter in a séance with trance medium Gladys Osborne Leonard. Feda, Leonard's control, was relaying messages from Raymond in spirit to Sir Oliver when Sir Oliver asked about the unknown group photograph. Raymond, through Feda, replied that the photograph was of a group of a dozen or more soldiers who were arranged close together in rows, with a seated front row and a back row. Feda went on to describe the photograph as having been taken outdoors but with a shelter and a black background with lines on its surface. One of the soldiers was leaning on Raymond's shoulder or trying to do so. Feda wanted Sir Oliver to note in particular that Raymond's walking stick was in the photograph.[61]

On December 7 the nine-by-twelve photo arrived at Sir Oliver's home. It shows a group of soldiers: five in the front row seated on grass, including Raymond, who has his walking stick; seven in the second row seated on chairs; and nine in the back row standing against the outside of a temporary wooden shed. The background is dark with notable vertical lines. Clearly, one of the soldiers sitting behind Raymond is leaning or resting a hand on Raymond's shoulder. Raymond appears annoyed by it. [62]

In the following photograph, an arrow points to Raymond in the front row, second from the right, seated on the ground.

Group photo with Raymond, his walking stick, and a hand on his left shoulder

Most remarkably, the existence of the photograph had come through two mediums independently.

In other communications, Raymond showed he was aware of what was going on in his father's life.

He referred to "a Roland for your Oliver," meaning that there had been a recent marriage resulting in a son-in-law named Roland.[63]

He came through in a séance with Gladys Osborne Leonard attended by his father on September 15, 1915, explaining what he meant in a September 27 séance with A. Vout Peters when he misspelled a location.[64]

In another séance with Leonard, Raymond through Feda described being with his father when his father was writing:

> "I am often with you, very often." [Raymond takes] Feda into a room with a desk in it; too big for a desk, it must be a table. A sort of a desk, a pretty big one. A chair is in front of it, not a chair like that, a high up chair, more wooden, not woolly stuff; and the light is falling on to the desk; and you are sitting there with a pen or pencil in your hand; you aren't writing much, but you are looking through writing, and making bits of writing on it; you are not doing all the writing yourself, but only bits on it. Raymond is standing at the back of you; he isn't looking at what you are doing.
>
> Oliver Lodge remarked, "The description is correct."[65]

In the same séance with Leonard, Raymond responded to Oliver Lodge's question about the "big bird" and "Mr. Jackson" by responding, "a fine bird" and "put him on a pedestal." Mr. Jackson was the name of Lady Lodge's peacock, which had just died. They were considering having a taxidermist stuff the bird. The peacock was to be mounted on a wooden pedestal.[66]

Evidence from Trance Mediumship Proves You Will Never Die

The details communicated about people's lives and current events verify that trance mediums are communicating with people living in the life after this life whose bodies have died. The communications demonstrate that people in spirit are aware of current efforts to prove the validity of their communications. In the examples cited, the people in spirit maintained regular, consistent communication about the locations of words and gave technical specifications of an airship. All the factual details conveyed articulately and without hesitation show that mediums communicated with people in the life after this life.

Evidence from communications through trance mediums with people whose bodies have died but are recognized by those who knew them proves you will never die.

Chapter 8

Communication through Automatic Writing Is Evidence You Will Never Die

Mediums receive messages from people living in the next life through automatic writing and planchette writing. They are called "automatists" and their writing is "automatization" or "psychography." In the purest form of automatic writing, the medium's arm and hand muscles are controlled by the person in spirit. The penmanship often matches that of the person in spirit while on earth. Talented automatists like Leonora Piper are able to write for two entities, one through each hand, while conversing about topics unrelated to the writing of either hand.

Automatic writing differs from "inspirational writing," in which the individual controls the writing and scribbles the words that come to mind. Whereas inspirational writing is often referred to as "automatic writing," the phenomenon is different.

In planchette writing, the medium or a small number of sitters place their fingertips on a flat piece of wood shaped like a heart elongated toward the point, called a "planchette." The device was first used for planchette writing and later used with the Ouija board. The planchette is perched on short dowels of wood like stilts that enable it to glide easily when nudged. A pencil inserted vertically in the pointed end makes contact with the paper to facilitate writing. The medium or sitters allow the planchette to move where it will to create the planchette writing.

Cross Correspondence

One form of communication coming through automatists that demonstrates the survival of consciousness is called "cross correspondence." A series of messages is given by people in the life after this life to two or more mediums in different parts of the world. The messages can be the same, or in pieces so that they convey a clear message only when combined. The involvement of several mediums precludes the possibility that a single medium is receiving psychic information rather than messages from people alive in spirit. A living person is required to carefully plan and convey a coherent message to a number of mediums.

1. The Mary Catherine Lyttelton Case

Mary Catherine Lyttelton was in a loving relationship with Arthur James Balfour but fell ill and died on March 21, 1875, before Balfour could propose marriage to her. Over the next thirty years, thousands of messages came from numerous mediums. Although meaningless in themselves, when considered as a whole they indicated that Lyttelton was trying to communicate with Balfour.[67] Because none of the mediums knew about the couple's relationship, inspiration by Lyttleton in spirit seemed credible. Each message contained repeated symbolic references to the pair.

> Lyttelton was figured, for instance, as a Palm Maiden (she passed on Palm Sunday), as Dante's Beatrice (whose "emerald eyes" stood for the ring in which Lyttelton was buried), and as the ancient queen Berenice (who dedicated her hair to a temple; Balfour had preserved a lock of Lyttelton's hair). Symbols for Arthur Balfour included a loyal knight, the *Idylls'* King Arthur, and verses from *Ode on the Death of the Duke of Wellington* by Alfred Tennyson, who had been Balfour's godfather and namesake.[68]

The communication amounted to what Balfour dubbed "a love story transcending life and death."[69] The fact that the correspondence came through several mediums demonstrates that Lyttleton was alive and capable of distributing the messages among mediums.

2. The Myers Cross Correspondence Case

The Myers Cross Correspondence is the best-known example of such communication. Frederick W. H. Myers, a Cambridge classics scholar and writer in the nineteenth century, was one of the founders of the Society for Psychical Research. He originated the concept of cross correspondence, calling it "concordant automatism" because it comes through automatic writers.

Two years after Myers's passing into spirit, Helen Verrall, an automatist, produced messages from Myers. Independently, Alice Fleming (sister of Rudyard Kipling), then living in India, received a message through automatic writing urging her to get in touch with Verrall and giving Verrall's address in Cambridge. Another significant automatist of this period was a sister-in-law of Myers, Winifred Coombe-Tennant, who also received messages from Myers. Automatist Rosina Thompson and the talented American medium Leonora Piper became involved when their automatic writing contained statements by Myers at the same time as messages were appearing in scripts by other automatists. None of these mediums possessed significant knowledge of Greek or Latin, yet the messages given to various mediums had Greek or Latin words in them.[70]

The messages were unintelligible individually but, over a long period and many séances, a purpose in the correspondences became apparent, indicating some individual in spirit was behind them. Alice Johnson, research officer of the Society for Psychical Research in London, first encountered the idea when messages were received through various mediums at about the same time in places as far apart as India, New York, and London. In the scripts of Rosina Thompson, Mrs. Forbes, Margaret Verrall (Helen Verrall's mother), and others, Johnson found fragmentary utterances that had no point or meaning, but when put together like a jigsaw puzzle formed coherent ideas.[71]

For example, in India on January 17, 1904, Alice Fleming recorded a message through automatic writing she said came from Myers: I Corinthians 16: 13. He told her that he'd tried to give her the verse in Greek but could not get her hand to form Greek characters, so he gave only the reference. That same day, thousands of miles away in England, Margaret Verrall received the same biblical reference from Myers via automatic writing. The verse, "Watch ye, stand fast in the faith, quit you like men...," was inscribed in Greek over the gateway of Selwyn College, Cambridge, under which Myers frequently walked.[72]

Later two other leaders of the Society for Psychical Research passed into spirit: Henry Sidgwick and Edmund Gurney. Soon after each of their transitions, they sent fragments of messages to mediums around the world and the Myers concordant automatism phenomenon was replicated successfully. Over the next thirty years more than three thousand such scripts were transmitted to mediums around the world, some as long as forty typed pages. They now fill twenty-four volumes of twelve thousand pages. As investigators involved in the research passed away, they joined the study on the other side by communicating incomplete messages through a number of mediums around the world that formed complete wholes when brought together. [73]

Hundreds of other accounts of cross correspondence are recorded in the *Proceedings of the Society for Psychical Research*.

> Taken as a whole, the Cross Correspondences and the Willett scripts are among the most convincing evidence that at present exists for "life after death." For anyone who is

prepared to devote weeks to studying them, they prove beyond all reasonable doubt that Myers, Gurney and Sidgwick went on communicating after death.[74]

Evidence of Communication through Automatic Writing Proves You Will Never Die

The clever, well-thought-out inspirations of mediums by people in spirit to form whole messages when brought together demonstrates that the communicators were alive, intelligent, and aware of current affairs on earth.

The evidence of cross-correspondence messages from people whose bodies have died to an assortment of mediums proves you will never die.

Chapter 9

Communication through Mental Mediumship Is Evidence You Will Never Die

Talented mental mediums are connecting people with their loved ones living in the next life. Many audio and video recordings of mediums in a variety of circumstances describe the intimate details and moving messages coming from loved ones. The details are known only to the person being read, or unknown even to that person but later verified.

Controlled experiments validating mental mediums' capabilities have been carried out by Gary Schwartz, Julie Beischel and Mark Boccuzzi of the Windbridge Institute, Tricia Robertson and Archie Roy, Donna Smith-Moncrieffe, Emily Kelly, and Diane Arcangel. On the whole, the research demonstrates that mediums acquire information about sitters and their loved ones in spirit that could not be reasonably guessed or acquired through research.

1. Canyon Ranch Experiment

To determine whether mediums do receive accurate information from people whose bodies have died, Gary Schwartz, Linda Russek, and Christopher Barentsen conducted a study for the Human Energy Systems Laboratory at the University of

Arizona. Their controlled experiment tested three talented mediums—Laurie Campbell, John Edward, and Suzane Northrop—at the Canyon Ranch in Tucson, Arizona.

The study revealed that the mediums identified details about deceased loved ones at a rate much higher than chance, leading the researchers to conclude that "The findings appear to confirm the hypothesis that information and energy, and potentially consciousness itself, can continue after physical death."[75]

2. Study for an HBO Documentary

Gary Schwartz performed a second study with three other researchers from the University of Arizona Human Energy Systems Laboratory for a video-recorded HBO documentary on the life after this life. The study used five well-known mediums: George Anderson, John Edward, Anne Gehman, Suzane Northrop, and Laurie Campbell.

The result was that the mediums' average accuracy score was 83 percent for one subject and 77 percent for a second subject. To test whether guessing could achieve the same results by chance, 68 control people were asked to guess details about the deceased loved ones of the two subjects. Their scores averaged 36 percent hits by chance. In other words, the accuracy of the mediums' details was far beyond chance guesses.[76]

3. The Miraval Silent-Sitter Experiment

The Miraval experiment involved mediums Suzane Northrop, John Edward, Anne Gehman, and Laurie Campbell and ten subjects. The study consisted of two parts for each reading with each subject. The first part was "silent"—the medium described details about the deceased without receiving any responses from the subject. In the second part, the medium received "yes" and "no" answers from the subject.

The mediums' accuracy score was 77 percent during the silent period and 85 percent during the "yes" and "no" questioning period, showing again that the mediums were far more accurate than would be expected by chance (based on the 36 percent accuracy rating in the previous study's control group).[77]

4. More Stringent Studies at the University of Arizona

Gary Schwartz and Julie Beischel performed another study under even more stringent, triple-blind conditions with more mediums. In this study the subjects weren't present for the reading. Another person sat in as a "proxy sitter." The readings were conducted by phone to eliminate even the presence of the proxy sitter with the medium. Eight mediums were involved to increase the validity of the data.

The result was that the average summary rating for the readings actually intended for the subject was 3.56 on a 6-point scale. The average summary ratings for the readings not intended for the person (that were actually readings for someone else) was 1.94. For three of the best-performing mediums, the summary scores were in the range of 5.0 to 5.5 out of 6, meaning they were dramatically accurate.[78]

A list of recommended, legitimate mediums, some of whom do phone readings, is at www.afterlifeinstitute.org/connect-loved-one-spirit/.

Evidence from Mental Mediumship Communication Proves You Will Never Die

Accounts of mental mediums' evidential mediumship readings are common. The readings have great face validity: the details the mediums provide could not be guessed or researched. The evidence from connections mental mediums are making with people whose bodies have died proves you will never die.

Chapter 10

Communication Experiences in Dreams Are Evidence You Will Never Die

People commonly experience visitations by loved ones when they are in a dream state. When the body and conscious mind are relaxed, people living in the life after this life can project images and conversations into the person's open, receptive mind. The experiencer's preoccupied, guarded conscious awareness is asleep, so the images and conversations provided by the person in the next life register and are remembered. The phenomena are called "dream visitations."

1. Edgar Cayce and Dream Visitations

Edgar Cayce, the renowned "sleeping prophet," believed that dream appearances of loved ones are intended to teach the dreamer something valuable about the person's life.

> Dreams, visions, impressions, to the entity in the normal sleeping state are the presentations of the experiences necessary for the development, if the entity would apply them in the physical life. These may be taken as warnings, as advice, as conditions to be met, conditions to be viewed in a way and manner as lessons, as truths, as they are presented in the various ways and manners.[79]

2. Dream Visitations When the Dreamer Learns Things He or She Could Not Have Known

In dream visitations, those communicating with people living in the life after this life often learn things they could not have known. The following account of a dream after-death communication (ADC) came from a patient of Dr. Allan Botkin, former psychotherapist with a large Chicago area VA hospital.[80] It illustrates the striking reality of the communication for the experiencer. You can listen to a narration of the text at www.afterlifeinstitute.org/jerry/.

> Jerry had come to see me for psychotherapy about an unrelated matter, but after developing some trust in me, felt he could tell me his spontaneous ADC story "without being labeled a nutcase." Jerry was living in the Midwest and his ex-wife was living on the East Coast with their three children. One night, he experienced the clear image of his ex-wife while he was asleep. "She looked beautiful, peaceful and happy," he said, "and she wanted to tell me about something of great concern to her." Jerry said she told him that he needed to start playing a more important role in rearing their children and even offered very specific suggestions about each child. Jerry said his experience was much clearer than a dream.
>
> Jerry awoke right after his experience, baffled by its remarkable clarity. He could remember the entire experience, and for him it felt like a real conversation with his ex-wife. After lying awake awhile trying to make sense of his experience, he managed to get back to sleep.
>
> The next morning as he was making coffee, the phone rang. It was his ex-wife's sister. Tearfully, she told Jerry his ex-wife had been killed in a car accident during the night.

> Suddenly, the meaning of his experience became clear. Since then, Jerry's ex-wife has appeared to him five times in spontaneous ADCs, each time offering further advice about their children. "Every time," he said, "she did all the talking." And after each experience, Jerry followed her advice closely. In all instances, the advice turned out to be very helpful.
>
> As he told me [Dr. Botkin] the story, Jerry laughed at one point and said "She hasn't changed much. She was always hyper-verbal and bossy." When I asked him if he thought that his wife had really visited him after she died, he said defiantly, "I am sure of it. I am as sure of it as I am that I'm looking at you right now. Nobody can ever tell me that it wasn't real, not you or anyone else. I don't care what other people think about this because they really don't know. I didn't believe in this stuff before it happened, but now I have no doubt whatsoever."[81]

One caregiver had just returned home exhausted from caring for her dying mother at a nursing home. She had a dream experience that occurred at the moment of her mother's transition without her realizing her mother had transitioned.

> My mother had been very ill for some time.... After dinner with my husband and children, I went to bed. During the middle of the night, I awoke from a very deep sleep. I had dreamed my mother had come to visit me. In this dream, she was with my father who had passed 5 years ago. Both of them looked happy and healthy. My mother blew me a kiss. Then she and my father turned around and walked off, over a hill. When I awoke, tears filled my eyes, but I also felt a sense of peace. My parents had looked so joyful. I looked at the clock and noted it was 3 a.m., then lay back down and went to sleep. The next morning my brother

called to tell me my mother had left us. When I asked him about the time of her death, he replied she had passed at 3 a.m.[82]

3. The Nature of Dreams and the Afterlife Communication Experience

According to dream researcher Claudia Carlton Lambright, dream visitations can be clear, recalled in vivid detail, and contain messages the visitor would characteristically have given to the dreamer.[83]

> I hope I'm adequately expressing how amazing this dream experience was—it was as if there were a play in progress, and I stepped onto the stage and asked one of the actors to hug me in the middle of the play! My family was going about their day as if nothing was unusual…but, it was a *dream,* and I was the only one who knew it.[84]

The vivid, natural quality of the dream and the fact that it is recalled in detail after the experience are the characteristics of a dream visitation. The dreams also contain statements the dreamer would not have originated. Claudia Carlton Lambright's account of her dream visitation follows. You can listen to a narration of the account at www.afterlifeinstitute.org/claudia/.

> Exactly a year after Rusty's death, he came to me in a very special dream. I dreamed I was at a business meeting. After getting checked in and moving into my hotel room, I went down to the lobby. There were lots of people there but they all seemed to be engaged in conversation, so I stayed in the fringes. Suddenly, I looked slightly to the right and there was Rusty, standing very close to me and smiling. I knew immediately that it was a "visit." Surprised and elated as usual, I cried, "Rusty, you're here!" "Yes," he said, "I felt you

really needed me, so I came." I think he asked me what's wrong, why was I pulling on him so hard. I told him I missed him and wanted to see him. He said, "Do you need help with the questions? If they ask you what's the most important thing, tell them 'kindness,' because it's not at all forthcoming." I hoped I would be able to remember everything he was saying. Then our son was there with us and the three of us were standing close together, holding hands. Then my consciousness faded and I opened my eyes, back in bed.[85]

Evidence from Dream Communications Proves You Will Never Die

People have dreams they describe as clear, unmistakable encounters with people whose bodies have died, and during the dream they learn things they could not have known or they have experiences not characteristic of them. This is evidence that people live on after their bodies die, proving you will never die.

Chapter 11

People's Common Afterlife Communication Experiences Are Evidence You Will Never Die

1. Studies of the Prevalence of Afterlife Communications Show They Are Common

Experiencing the presence of loved ones living in the life after this life is common. In a study reported in the *American Journal of Psychiatry*, two-thirds of those surveyed in the U.S. had sensed the presence of the person who had transitioned to the next life.[86] The experience can hardly be called unusual.

In 1987 the Gallup Organization published the results of a survey designed to find out how many people had after-death communication experiences of any kind in Britain. The survey showed that 48 percent of those asked felt they were personally aware of this kind of experience in their lives.[87]

A broad range of studies of communication with people living in the life after this life have shown that such communication is common.[88]

> Rees found that 50 percent of widowers reported visions of departed spouses that occurred to them while in the waking state.[89] Holden reported that 70 percent to 80 percent of widows and widowers had such visions.[90]

Haraldsson, in a national survey in Iceland, reported that 31 percent of respondents reported <u>visual</u> encounters with loved ones living in the life after this life.[91]

Kalish studied adults in Los Angeles and found that 55 percent of blacks, 54 percent of Mexican-Americans, 38 percent of Anglo-Americans, and 29 percent of Japanese-Americans reported such encounters.[92]

These experiences have also been reported in traditional Hopi Indians.[93]

In 1988, Bill and Judy Guggenheim began The ADC Project, in which they interviewed 3,300 people who had experienced communication with people living in the life after this life. The accounts were emotional, heartwarming, and at times startling. They describe them in their book, *Hello from Heaven*,[94] which includes 353 of the stories they heard. Reading the clear, heartfelt stories by ordinary people who insist they communicated with their loved ones in the life after this life cannot help but convince all but the most hardened skeptics that our loved ones are alive, well, and close by after leaving the body, just in a different form.

The number of people who have had such experiences with loved ones in the life after this life is increasing, in part because of the openness to the phenomenon today. Communication with loved ones now living in the life after this life is a common, everyday occurrence. People don't talk about their communication experiences because of the odd notion in our culture that if we talk about such experiences, people will think we're delusional. But if you bring up the subject of near-death experiences or communication with loved ones in the life after this life in a group and let people know it's OK to talk about them, the stories start to roll out.

2. People Communicating with Those in the Next Life Learn Things They Couldn't Know Otherwise

It is common for people communicating with someone living in the life after this life to receive messages about things they could not have known. This could not happen if the messages had not come from a person living there. In one case, a woman's life was saved by someone whose identity she learned later.

> In some cases people appear apparently with the express purpose of saving loved ones from danger. This happened to Elaine Worrell who lived with her husband Hal on the top floor of an apartment building in Oskaloosa, Iowa. One day she saw a young man in her hallway who led her downstairs into the apartment of a young widow whom she barely knew. She found the young woman collapsed on a bed after having slashed her wrists. After she recovered, the young woman showed Elaine a photograph of her late husband; Elaine recognized it immediately as the young man who had led her downstairs and into the apartment.[95]

3. Pre-death and Deathbed Visions of Loved Ones Living in the Life after This Life Are Common

Our Universal Intelligence has created conditions in the days and hours at the end of this life so the transition into the next plane of eternal life is as comfortable as possible. Pre-death visions are an example of the preparation for a gentle, loving transition.

Pre-death visions are visions of deceased loved ones that patients commonly have in the weeks before they die. *Deathbed visions* are the visions dying patients have in the days or hours immediately preceding death. They are counselors bringing reassurance and peace to those about to make the transition.

Dr. James L. Hallenbeck, the director of palliative care services with the Veterans Administration Palo Alto Health Care System, estimates that pre-death visions or deathbed visions occur prior to at least 25 percent of deaths.[96] Some estimate this number even higher. Of the 10 percent of dying people who are conscious shortly before their deaths, between 50 and 60 percent experience deathbed visions.[97]

Children are truth-tellers because of their youthful naïveté, so when they experience such visions they describe them matter-of-factly. Pre-death and deathbed vision stories are common among children. A pediatrician described them as astonishing scientific proof of the validity of the near-death experience.[98]

A Yale pediatric oncologist described a seven-year-old girl who sat up in bed just before her death from leukemia and said, "The angels, they are so beautiful, can't you hear them singing, Mommy?" A boy dying of leukemia said God spoke to him and that he asked God if he could live another year so he could explain his death to his three-year-old brother. Amazingly, against medical odds, the boy lived one more year.[99]

A healthy four-year-old girl had a vivid dream she described to her mother. She said she saw a beautiful golden heaven and that it was "really, really, real," with gold angels, diamonds, and jewels. It was a fun place. There, she met Jesus. She told her mother not to worry because Jesus would take care of her. She then went out to play and sadly was murdered only hours later.[100]

In 1959, Dr. Karlis Osis, a psychology professor at the University of Freiburg, and Dr. Erlendur Haraldsson, a psychology professor at the University of Munich, studied deathbed visions in the U.S. and India by interviewing doctors and nurses who had been present when people died. The responses from doctors and nurses indicated that over 1,300 dying patients saw apparitions and almost 900 reported visions of the life after this life. The following were common in these visions:

- Some people reported seeing angels and other religious figures, but most saw familiar deceased people.
- Very often friends and relatives communicated that they had come to help take the person away.
- The person was reassured by the experience, expressed great happiness, and was quite willing to go with the deceased greeters.
- The person's mood and health often changed during and after the vision, elating the once depressed or relieving the suffering of those in pain.
- The person was acutely aware of his or her real surroundings and conditions, not immersed in a fantasy.
- The experience and reactions afterward were the same for all experiencers, whether or not they believed in a life after this life.[101]

Osis and Haraldsson concluded that the death-bed visions of both countries support the assertion that people continue to live after bodily death.[102]

Carla Wills-Brandon is a licensed marriage and family therapist and author of nine books exploring addiction, self-esteem, sexual trauma, death, the life after this life, and spirituality. After sitting up all night with his father in the hospital, her husband told her of his experience of a deathbed vision.

> Tonight while snoozing in the chair in his room, I had a wonderful dream about Da. In this dream he said to me he was going soon, but that he would always watch over us.

> Upon awakening, I looked over at Da as he slept and noticed he was very at ease. Suddenly, I saw something rise from his body. It was absolutely beautiful. A whirl of pastel color, vibrant in not only appearance but also movement, was leaving his chest area. It was so comforting." The following week, Da gently passed away in my husband's arms.[103]

Many caregivers have similar experiences at the bedsides of people passing.[104] Countless hospice workers have seen a wisp of something leave the body at the moment of death, and patients commonly describe visions of deceased relatives, angels, or celestial beings of light. The caregivers themselves often describe receiving visits during dreams from deceased relatives or even the dying person.

In his studies of end-of-life phenomena, neuroscientist Dr. Peter Fenwick, fellow of the Royal College of Psychiatrists, discovered a woman who witnessed the spiritual image of her husband's transition:

> Suddenly there was the most brilliant light shining from my husband's chest, and as this light lifted upward, there was the most beautiful music and singing voices. My own chest seemed filled with infinite joy, and my heart felt as if it was lifting to join this light and music. Suddenly, there was a hand on my shoulder, and a nurse said, "Sorry, love. He's just gone." I lost sight of the light and the music and felt so bereft at being left behind.[105]

Deathbed visions are quite common and are not explained by any medical or psychological influence. Those on the next plane of life are helping the dying person make the transition.

View a video of Dr. Martha Jo Atkins, LPC-S and founder of the Death and Dying Institute, describing near-death and deathbed visions: www.earthschoolanswers.com/atkins/.

View a video of Dr. Christopher Kerr, the chief medical officer of the Hospice & Palliative Care Buffalo Research Department, describing dreams dying people have about family members, and interviewing them as they describe their own dreams: www.earthschoolanswers.com/kerr/.

Evidence from Common Afterlife Communication Proves You Will Never Die

The evidence that afterlife communication is commonplace and widely acknowledged by people proves that people live on after their bodies die and are able to communicate to show they are alive. Pre-death and deathbed visions are common. The people living in the life after this life are communicating with dying people who knew them on earth, proving that you will not die when your body dies.

Second Area of Evidence You Will Never Die

The Nature of Reality and Consciousness Described by Science

The next four chapters of this book provide evidence in four areas that your mind survives bodily death—you will never die.

1. You are a manifestation of Our Universal Intelligence that will never die
2. Your mind is not in your brain, so the death of your brain has no effect on your mind

3. Near-death experiences show the person's mind at the approach of the transition becomes more aware and calm rather than confused and agitated.

4. Researchers, scientists, and other highly regarded professionals who study consciousness and the survival of consciousness after bodily death have concluded people survive bodily death.

The evidence in these four chapters proves that your mind, integral with Our Universal Intelligence, has all the properties scientists and researchers have identified that demonstrate you will live on after your body and brain die.

Chapter 12

Evidence You Are a Manifestation of Our Universal Intelligence that Will Never Die

Materialists assert that consciousness is secreted by the brain just as adrenaline is secreted by the adrenal glands, so when the brain dies, consciousness dies. Reality, they assert, is composed of objects in space and time that exist independent of consciousness. Consciousness evolved by chance from the outworking of physical laws and natural selection.

The materialists are mistaken. Consciousness is the basis of reality. The underlying source of reality is Our Universal Intelligence. What we see as matter and energy are experiences in consciousness. Experiences come into awareness briefly and are replaced by new experiences; they are transient. But we are permanent. We are the consciousness that is aware of the experiences. As a result, when our body dies the experiences in consciousness change but our consciousness remains alive.

Your mind will never die because you are an individual member of Our Universal Intelligence that is creating this reality. You are not a body and brain in a world that is an accident in time outside of Our Universal Intelligence. Because you are part of Our Universal Intelligence, you are creating a world of experiences that is a temporary dream, but you the dreamer will never die.

1. Quantum Mechanics

At the heart of quantum mechanics is the wave-particle duality. It suggests that what we experience as reality is in probability waves until we observe or measure it. The waves are only probabilities that objects could be what we will experience when we observe the objects. The objects don't exist until we observe them. At the observation, the probabilities collapse and one experience out of the many possibilities becomes our experience of reality. In other words, reality is mind-dependent, or isn't there until we experience it.[106]

The following prominent scientists and researchers support this view of the nature of reality.

Dr. Bruce Rosenblum and Dr. Fred Kuttner, physics professors at the University of California at Santa Cruz: "The object was not there before you found it there."[107]

Dr. Anton Zelinger, Austrian quantum physicist, professor of physics at the University of Vienna, and senior scientist at the Institute for Quantum Optics and Quantum Information at the Austrian Academy of Sciences: "Rather than passively observing it, we are in fact creating reality."[108]

Dr. Bernard Haisch, astrophysicist, president of the Digital Universe Foundation, and professor of physical science, math, and engineering at Foothill College in Los Altos, California: "It's consciousness that is the ultimate reality out of which everything else has come."[109]

Sir James Jeans, pioneering physicist and mathematician and professor at the University of Cambridge and Princeton University: "The Universe begins to look more like a great thought than like a great machine. Mind no longer appears to be an accidental intruder into the realm of matter ... we ought rather hail it as the creator and governor of the realm of matter."[110]

Werner Heisenberg, German theoretical physicist who was one of the key pioneers of quantum mechanics: "The idea of an objective real world... is impossible.... The transition from the 'possible' to the 'actual' takes place during the act of observation."[111]

John Wheeler, American theoretical physicist and professor of physics at Princeton University: "No elementary quantum phenomenon is a phenomenon until it is an... observed... phenomenon."[112]

Andrew Truscott, Australian National University professor of atomic and molecular physics: "At the quantum level, reality does not exist if you are not looking at it."[113]

You are not a passive observer of a world of matter and energy outside of you that happens to you. There is only your mind and your experiences in Our Universal Intelligence. We experience the world in our minds, which are individual members of Our Universal Intelligence. Our reality is created in the same way a memory is created, brought to our minds when we want and expect it by Our Universal Intelligence. We are experiencing a world that becomes experiences for us when we expect them. The world doesn't exist until we have the experiences of sight, sound, touch, taste, or smell given by Our Universal Intelligence. We are not in bodies and brains that would exist if we were not there to observe them. We are Our Universal Intelligence, which has no beginning or ending and will never cease to exist. You will never cease to exist. You will never die.

For more on this, read *There Is Nothing but Mind and Experiences*.[114]

2. Experiences as the Content of Reality

Matter and energy do not create mind. Mind creates the experiences of matter and energy. When your mind experiences a sight, sound, touch, taste, or smell, the experiences are coming from Our Universal Intelligence that we are all part of. There is no objective reality outside of your mind that we perceive from energy entering tiny orifices in a material body.

It's like we're having a dream. When we dream, we experience people, scenery, and events. We also have a dream self in the dream. The dream seems real. We act in it as though it were real. But the dream is only in our minds.

We aren't creating the dream. Our Universal Intelligence is giving us our dream self, the characters, the scenery, and the events just as Our Universal Self is giving us the Earth School realm we are living in.

If I see a red chair in my dream, there is no chair there. There is only the experience of a red chair in my mind. But I have the feeling in the dream that there really is a red chair outside of me. I might walk to it and touch it. I might sit on it and move it. I might invite other characters in my dream to sit on it. But it's only the experience of a red chair. There's no red chair there. There is no photograph of a red chair, no holograph, and no projection of a red chair. There is only the experience of a red chair, but I experience it fully. Experiences exist in dreams without objects to be sensed outside of us.

In our daily lives we are having experiences without objects in a world around us. We have them together because we are one mind, Our Universal Intelligence. At each moment, we are being given one experience that is experienced by many individuals. We each then take away from the experience what is relevant to us. What we notice becomes a memory unique for each of us. Extending the chair example from the dream into our waking world, when you and I see a chair as we enter a room together, you may notice the upholstery of the chair and I remember the shape of the back. The image of the upholstery and back and all the other dozens of aspects of the chair were in the experiences available to us in Our Universal Intelligence, but the memory that became part of our repertoire of memories was of what was noteworthy or important to each of us. We have access to all the dozens of aspects of the experience of the chair, but we come away with memories of only those aspects of the chair we noticed.

The dream world and the "real" world are just experiences in Our Universal Intelligence. In the same way, imagination and remembering result from asking Our Universal Intelligence for the experiences of novel thought or remembered images, sounds, and other sensory experiences. Our Universal Intelligence is providing a reality for us wholly in our minds in the dream, or when we are remembering, or when we are imagining a sensory experience, or when we are having experiences in Earth School. Our Universal Intelligence is giving us experiences without our effort in all these states of mind. All are happening in our mind, where the only reality resides.

3. Near-Death Experiences of Blind People

One of the proofs that there are only experiences in our minds, with no world outside of us, is that blind people, including those blind from birth, can see clearly during near-death experiences (NDEs) and out-of-the-body experiences (OBEs), demonstrating that their minds must be having sight experiences independent of their sight-impaired bodies.

Dr. Kenneth Ring, professor emeritus of psychology at the University of Connecticut, and Sharon Cooper interviewed thirty-one blind and sight-impaired persons who had had NDEs and OBEs. Ring and Cooper found that 80 percent of the individuals reported visual experiences correctly, including colors and details in their surroundings. One patient who had been totally blind for forty years had the experience of seeing the pattern and colors on a new tie during an OBE, even though everyone denied having ever described it to him. They published the results of the two-year research study in the book *Mindsight*.[115]

The fact that the research subjects were blind meant they could not have had sight experiences if they were relying on a world around them for experiences. It could only happen if sight experiences are in the mind, and when the mind is freed from the constraints of the body, the mind has vivid sight experiences.

These blind people had sensory experiences in their minds because, while their bodies were unconscious, their minds were unimpeded by their bodies' blindness. When they were no longer following the set of rules in their body experience, they had visual experiences with great acuity, but without relying on objects outside of themselves because they were blind and unconscious.

Evidence That You Are Our Universal Intelligence Proves You Will Never Die

Quantum mechanics physicists tell us that there is no reality apart from our sensory experiences. Until we have the experiences, there are only possibilities the experiences could be available. We are experiencing the world together, as though we were in the same dream. Evidence of that is the fact that blind people are able to see in NDEs although their bodies and brains have no access to sensory experience outside of them because they are blind. They have sight experiences, demonstrating that sight experiences and other experiences exist independent of a physical realm.

Beginnings and endings are part of the scenery in Earth School. They are artificial constructs. Our reality is the experiences we have in Our Universal Intelligence, not in a world outside of us that has beginnings and endings. As a result, there is nothing to die; we never die, even though our body experiences dying.

Chapter 13

Evidence Your Mind Is Not in Your Brain Means You Will Never Die

Advancements in humankind's knowledge about consciousness and the nature of reality have now provided evidence that while consciousness may have a relationship to the brain, it is not produced by the brain, is not housed in the brain, and functions perfectly well when the brain is not involved. As a result, you will live on after your brain dies. This chapter proves that this is true.

1. Researchers Cannot Find a Mind in the Brain and Cannot Explain How a Brain Creates a Mind

The brain has been carefully mapped using CTs, MRIs, fMRIs, PETs, and EEGs to identify which parts are active when a person is performing activities, engaging in mental functions, and experiencing sensory input. In spite of all the brain mapping that has been done, researchers cannot find localized areas of consciousness or memories in the brain. They also are unable to advance a viable explanation for how the brain could create consciousness. That is known as the "hard problem of consciousness."

The following scientists and researchers have discussed this.

Stephan Patt of the Institute of Pathology at Friedrich Schiller University in Germany: "All attempts which have been undertaken to specify the neurological mechanisms of consciousness in terms of neurobiological, information processing and even social theories of consciousness have failed to prove this causal relationship."[116]

Sir John Maddox, former editor-in-chief of the renowned journal *Nature*: "Despite the marvelous success of neuroscience in the past century, we seem as far from understanding cognitive processes as we were a century ago."[117]

Dr. David Presti, professor of neurobiology at the University of California, Berkeley: "At present, researchers and theorists do not understand the nature of the connection [between consciousness and patterns of cellular activity in the brain], the higher-order interpretation of physiological activities that produces mental experience."[118]

Dr. Stuart Hameroff, researcher in neuroscience and consciousness in the Department of Anesthesiology, Arizona Health Sciences Center: "What consciousness actually *is*, and how it comes about remain unknown."[119]

Dr. David J. Chalmers, former director of the Centre for Consciousness at the Australian National University: "Consciousness, the subjective experience of an inner self, could be a phenomenon forever beyond the reach of neuroscience. Even a detailed knowledge of the brain's workings and the neural correlates of consciousness may fail to explain how or why human beings have self-aware minds."[120]

2. Researchers and Scientists Have Begun to Suggest the Mind Is Not in the Brain

Researchers and scientists are not able to explain how the brain could produce consciousness, where consciousness is located, or how and where life memories are stored, even though the brain has been carefully studied and mapped. That has led them to look elsewhere for consciousness and memories.

The following scientists assert that consciousness has a relationship to the brain but is not dependent on it for its existence.

Dr. Stanislav Grof, Freudian psychoanalyst, assistant professor of psychiatry at Johns Hopkins University School of Medicine, and chief of psychiatric research at the Maryland Psychiatric Research Center: "Today, I came to the conclusion that [the mind] is not coming from the brain.... I don't think you can locate the source of consciousness. I am quite sure it is not in the brain—not inside of the skull."[121]

Sir John Eccles, internationally recognized brain scientist whose work has had a major influence on brain research: "The mind is a separate entity from the brain, and... mental processes cannot be reduced to neurochemical brain processes, but on the contrary direct them.... A mind may conceivably exist without a brain."[122]

Sir Cyril Burt, educational psychologist renowned for his studies on the effects of heredity on intelligence: "The brain is not an organ that generates consciousness, but rather an instrument evolved to transmit and limit the processes of consciousness and of conscious attention."[123]

Dr. Wilder Penfield, pioneering Canadian neuroscientist and brain surgeon who operated on over a thousand epilepsy patients while they were awake under local anesthesia and believed that stimulation of no part of the brain could cause or impede any of the actions associated with the mind: "The intellect and the will are not from the brain."[124]

Dr. Sam Parnia, physician at Southampton General Hospital, England: " When we examine brain cells we see that brain cells are like any other cells, they can produce proteins and chemicals, but they are not really capable of producing the subjective phenomenon of thought that we have."[125]

Dr. Subhash Kak, professor of quantum computing and neural networks, Oklahoma University; Dr. **Deepak Chopra,** board certified physician; and **Dr. Menas Kafatos,** quantum physicist and cosmologist at Chapman university: "We've proposed that consciousness creates reality and makes it knowable—if there's another viable candidate, it must pass the acid test: Transform itself into thoughts, feelings, images, and sensations. Science isn't remotely close to turning the sugar in a sugar bowl [the brain] into the music of Mozart or the plays of Shakespeare."[126]

3. The Brain Doesn't Have the Capacity to Hold a Lifetime of Memories

Dr. Simon Berkovich, American computer science expert, and **Dr. Herms Romijn,** Dutch brain researcher, working independently of one another, came to the conclusion that it is impossible for the brain to store everything a person thinks and experiences in a lifetime. "Simply watching an hour of television would already be too much for our brains."[127]

4. Psychics Know Information Not Available to Their Brains

Psychics know information they are not receiving from their body's senses. They could only receive it from a mind outside of the brain. For example, in an Australian series on psychic detectives, Debbie Malone and Scott Russell-Hill attempted to provide details about a case, knowing only that it was a murder. These are the details they correctly identified:

- The victim's gender: female

- The victim's name: Sarah
- The victim's age: early twenties
- The status of the body: still missing
- The general date of the murder: around thirteen years before (actually fifteen years)
- What the victim had been doing: coming home from tennis
- Where the victim was attacked: getting into her little red car
- The exact parking space used by the victim
- Other automobile involved: a cream-colored early 1980s Holden Commodore
- The area the murder took place: Frankston
- The specific location of the murder: Kananook
- The murder weapon: a knife
- The time of day: nighttime
- Whether there was more than one attacker: a group
- Characteristics of the group: there was a female member
- The nickname of a member of the group: "Dwarfie"
- The group leader's nickname: "Rat-head"
- The attacker's name
- Where there had been blood on the ground
- Where a witness who hadn't come forward had stood
- A map identical to the area concerned (drawn by Russell-Hill) [128]

The details were not available to the psychics' brains. They came to the mind that is outside of the brain.

In a different case, a psychic detective named Phil Jordan and the detectives involved appeared on a television show titled "Psychic Detectives"[129] in 2005. Two men had apparently drowned in a fast-moving stream in the Finger Lakes region of New York, but their bodies could not be found. Jordan saw in his mind's eye a red flower floating downstream where the body of the larger of the two men would be found, but flowers in late winter didn't seem possible. Jordan pinpointed pools of water on a map to indicate the location of the body.

The detectives found the pools and the larger man's body. They also found red flowers floating downstream. Friends of the deceased had dropped flowers into the water where the man probably fell in, as a memorial. The flowers had floated downstream to where the body was found.

Psychic activity in documented cases like these happens commonly today. Psychics use their minds to learn information they could not know if their minds were confined to brains inside the constraints of a skull.

5. The Mind Knows Information before the Brain Has Access to It

The mind knows information and registers it in the body before the brain is ever involved or has access to it. This is more evidence that the mind is outside of the brain.

Bodies React to Random Images before a Computer Selects Them

Dr. Dean Radin, senior scientist at the Institute of Noetic Sciences, performed carefully controlled studies in which people seated before a computer monitor were shown images. A computer selected at random and showed in random order either calm, pastoral scenes and neutral household objects or erotic and violent scenes. Radin continually measured participants' skin conductance levels, which, like a lie detector, show whether someone feels stress. As you might expect, participants showed stress at seeing the erotic and violent scenes and calm when shown the calm, pastoral scenes.

Remarkably, the tests consistently showed that some people had the appropriate reaction as early as six seconds before they saw a picture, even though the computer hadn't selected it yet. These people weren't using sensory organs to learn about the pictures.[130] They were not guessing, because their bodies were reacting but their minds had no part in making guesses. The person's mind must have already been having sight experiences and reacting to them before the information even existed in the physical realm for the eyes to see.

The studies were replicated by Dick Bierman, a psychologist at the University of Amsterdam and Utrecht University.[131]

People Successfully Predict Targets Before a Target Is Selected at Random

Other evidence demonstrates that the mind knows things before the brain is involved. Dr. Charles Honorton was director of the division of parapsychology and psychophysics at Maimonides Medical Center in New York. He and his colleagues examined the results of experiments designed to test "forced-choice precognition." In such experiments a subject was shown several "targets" (colored lamps, symbols on cards, or the number on a die) and asked to guess which one would be randomly chosen by a computer, by throwing a die, or by some other method no one could influence. The studies compared each subject's prediction with the randomly selected target.

Honorton and his colleagues studied the reports of 309 experiments, conducted by 62 different investigators, from 113 articles published from 1935 to 1987. The combined total was 2 million individual trials involving over 50,000 subjects. The time intervals between the guesses and the random selections of targets ranged from milliseconds to a year. The results showed that subjects were able to predict which target would be selected more often than would occur by chance guessing, with the odds against chance at ten trillion trillion to one.[132]

As might be expected, when these findings were published, other researchers in universities around the world, from Scotland's Edinburgh University to Cornell in the United States, rushed to duplicate the experiment and improve on it. They all got similar results and extended the experiments and findings:

> It was soon discovered that gamblers began reacting subconsciously shortly before they won or lost. The same effect was seen in those who are terrified of animals moments before they were shown the creatures. The odds against all of these trials being wrong is literally millions to one against.[133]

In other words, the mind outside the body knows information before the information is available for any of the body's senses or brain to receive it.

6. Consciousness Functions without Brain Involvement

Since researchers have been unsuccessful in finding the location of consciousness in the brain, we should expect to see evidence that consciousness functions without the brain's involvement. In fact, that is what occurs. Well-documented phenomena demonstrate that consciousness has experiences and acquires knowledge when the brain could not be involved.

Remote Viewers Have Sensory Experiences of Things Far Removed from Their Brains

When remote viewers sit quietly with their eyes closed and focus on something a mile or several thousand miles away, they have experiences of sight, sound, smell, taste, touch, movement, spatial perspective, and other senses. The person's consciousness is having sensory experiences without involvement of the brain or sensory organs.

For several decades at the end of the twentieth century, the CIA had a remote viewing program named Operation Stargate that attempted to use remote viewers to spy on the Russians. To evaluate the efficacy of the psychic activities, the CIA commissioned the Stanford Research Institute to perform 154 experiments with 26,000 separate trials over 16 years. At the end of that testing period, Dr. Edwin May, a researcher in low-energy experimental nuclear physics, headed a team of researchers that analyzed the experiments and reported to the government. They concluded that the odds against someone merely guessing what remote viewers had successfully described when focusing on a target at a distant location was more than a billion billion to one. His only explanation was that remote viewers genuinely have sensory experiences without using their sensory organs and without regard for how many miles away the target is.[134]

Congress and the CIA commissioned a study by the Science Applications International Corporation (SAIC). The result of the study was that Jessica Utts, professor in the Division of Statistics at the University of California, Davis, wrote, "It is clear to this author that anomalous cognition is possible and has been demonstrated. This conclusion is not based on belief, but rather on commonly accepted scientific criteria."[135]

The Princeton Engineering Anomalies Research (PEAR) laboratory began conducting independent studies of remote viewers in 1978. A person would travel to a distant, undisclosed location and the remote viewer would identify details about the location. In 334 trials, remote viewers successfully described details about the location with odds against guessing the details of one hundred billion to one.[136]

In another study, Robert Jahn, former director of the PEAR laboratory, and psychologist Brenda Dunne conducted 336 rigorous trials with 48 ordinary people who were asked to do remote viewing at distances ranging from five to six thousand miles. Almost two-thirds of the results were successful at rates that exceeded chance levels, with odds against chance being one billion to one.[137]

Russell Targ, the physicist who pioneered development of the laser, and Harold Puthoff, physicist and co-author of the widely read *Fundamentals of Quantum Electronics*, conducted experiments on remote viewing to determine its validity. In their tests a person they called a "beacon" traveled to a distant site to see whether a remote viewer could receive mental impressions about the site. The beacon and remote viewer were separated by distances of several miles so there could be no communication between them. The remote viewer was to focus on the beacon, trying to get impressions about where the beacon was and writing or sketching the scenes. They concluded, "Independent judges found that the descriptions of the sketches matched on the average 66 percent of the time the characteristics of the site that was actually seen by the beacon."[138]

The confirmed success of remote viewing demonstrates that a person can have sensory experiences with neither the sense organs nor the brain involved. Consciousness could only have these experiences if it is outside the brain and has functioning sensory sensitivities and memory without the involvement of sensory organs or the brain.

Examples of remote viewing are at www.afterlifeinstitute.org/rv/.

Removing Large Parts of the Brain Does Not Affect Consciousness

One of the explanations for the location of consciousness and memories in the brain is the "whole-brain" theory.[139] Because researchers cannot locate consciousness or memories in the brain, but an array of areas light up when consciousness is functioning, they theorize that since it can be found at no specific location it must be everywhere. However, the results of hemispherectomies belie that theory. A hemispherectomy removes half the brain from the patient's head to alleviate the debilitating effects of disorders that cannot be controlled using any other treatments. The consciousness of many people after this surgery functions normally, indicating that their minds must be viable without the need of both halves of the brain. A study of twenty-three hemispherectomy patients found that "Successful functional hemispherectomy significantly improved the cognitive function of patients."[140]

Some People with Little Brain Tissue Function Perfectly Well

Dr. John Lorber, professor of pediatrics at the University of Sheffield, examined the cases of a large number of people with hydrocephalus, in which the cranial cavity is filled with cerebrospinal fluid so only a thin layer of brain tissue exists. Among the patients having the most severe form of hydrocephalus, with most of their cranium filled with cerebrospinal fluid, many function perfectly normally despite the missing brain.

One student at the University of Sheffield had an IQ of 130 and verbal IQ of 140, gained a first-class honors degree in mathematics, and was socially completely normal, and yet had virtually no brain.

> When we did a brain scan on him ... we saw that instead of the normal 4.5-centimeter thickness of brain tissue between the

ventricles and the cortical surface, there was just a thin layer of mantle measuring a millimeter or so. His cranium is filled mainly with cerebrospinal fluid.[141]

View a video of Dr. Lorber describing the student at www.earthschoolanswers.com/roger/.

> Of the 687 patients whose brains Lorber scanned, 16 persons belonged to this group [extreme hydrocephalus], and half of them were regarded as cognitively normal—that is, they had an IQ of 100 or more."[142]

Another patient named Sharon had severe hydrocephalus, with virtually no brain tissue. In spite of that, she graduated from school, passing every examination she took, had more than average intelligence, and was the only girl in the school to receive a graduate certificate in chemistry and only one of two girls to receive one in biology.[143]

View a video of an interview with Sharon at www.earthschoolanswers.com/sharon/.

People Experiencing NDEs Have Sensory Experiences of Things Distant from Their Unconscious Bodies

People having near-death experiences (NDEs) often describe seeing and hearing things during the time their brains are incapacitated and they are comatose, with their eyes closed. Many of these experiences are of environments outside the room or building in which the person's body lies. During these episodes, the person's senses are acutely aware and memory functions perfectly so the sensory details of the excursion away from the body are recalled in exquisite detail.

Maria, a migrant worker, was brought to Harborview Medical Center's cardiac care unit in cardiac arrest, near death. After she was revived she told Kimberly Clark, M.S.W., who had been called to calm Maria's excitement, that while she was unconscious she felt herself floating upward out of the hospital. As she rose, she saw, on a third-story window ledge of the hospital, "a man's dark blue tennis shoe, well-worn, scuffed on the left side where the little toe would go. The shoelace was caught under the heel." Kimberly searched the ledges of the hospital windows and was surprised to find a tennis shoe precisely where Maria had described it. The shoe was dark blue, had a well-worn scuff on the left side where the little toe would go, and the shoelace was caught under the heel.[144]

In another incident, after an unconscious patient was revived, she described floating above the hospital, where she saw a red tennis shoe on the roof. A janitor investigated and found a red tennis shoe just where the patient described.[145]

In both instances the patients were incapacitated, so their brains were not functioning sufficiently to have sensory experiences. They both had accurate sight experiences of shoes whose sight would have been inaccessible to them even if they had been able to see and process sights during their NDE. Their experiences indicate that their minds were not in their brains.

For a more detailed examination of the evidence that consciousness is not dependent on the brain, read *Your Eternal Self: Science Discovers the Afterlife*.[146]

7. People Commonly Describe Separating the Mind from the Body in Out-of-Body Experiences

In out-of-body experiences (OBEs), people describe being conscious outside of their bodies and having normal sensory experiences, such as traveling to locations, listening to conversations, and seeing distant people while the body is motionless. OBEs are surprisingly common. Five surveys done in the United Sates dating back to 1954 show that as high as 25 percent of those polled responded that they had experienced an OBE. A 1975 survey of a randomly selected group of 1,000 students and townspeople in a small town in Virginia found that 25 percent of the students and 14 percent of the townspeople reported having had an OBE.[147]

Reports of OBEs have been well-documented for centuries. Fredric Myers's book, *Human Personality and Its Survival of Bodily Death*, documents hundreds of carefully recorded and verified accounts of OBEs.[148]

In May 1980, Dr. Glen Gabbard of the Menninger Foundation, Dr. Stewart Twemlow of the Topeka VA Medical Center, and Dr. Fowler Jones of the University of Kansas Medical Center presented the findings of studies of OBEs to the American Psychiatric Association's annual meeting in San Francisco. The researchers reported that those who experience OBEs describe them as being distinctly different from dreams or hallucinations. They describe feeling a real sense of separation of the mind from the body. The experiencers in the study tested normal in all psychological and physical senses.[149]

D. Scott Rogo examined over 60 studies of OBEs and found these common conclusions:

- The OBE experience is a common human experience, with roughly 10 to 20 percent of the adult population experiencing an OBE sometime in their lives.

- OBE experiencers aren't special types of persons (e.g., persons with pathological states of mind, overanxious about death, or prone to fantasy).

- At least some OBE experiencers can be "detected" at distant locations during their OBE travels by the use of animal, human, and sometimes physical detectors.

- At least some gifted OBE experiencers can make surprisingly correct observations at distant locations while traveling out of the body.

- At least some OBEs are certainly not dreams or hallucinations.[150]

OBEs demonstrate the fact that the mind is not confined to the brain.

8. Biophysicists Can Detect No Electrical Activity in Sensory Neurons That Have Been Assumed to Carry Sensory Information

Attempts to measure electricity along the sensory neurons when a person is apparently sensing something have failed to find traces of it. The laws of thermodynamics dictate that electrical impulses must produce heat. Thomas Heimburg, associate professor of biophysics at the Niels Bohr Institute at Copenhagen University, and Andrew D. Jackson, professor of theoretical physics at Copenhagen University, attempted to detect heat from the electricity when impulses are traveling along nerves to produce sensory experiences. They found none.

Medical and biological textbooks all state that nerves function by sending electrical impulses along their length. Heimburg writes that their research shows the textbooks are wrong:

> But for us as physicists, this cannot be the explanation. The physical laws of thermodynamics tell us that electrical impulses must produce heat as they travel along the nerve, but experiments find that no such heat is produced...[151]

In other words, there appears to be no electrical activity coming from the sensory organs, although the brain does register electrical activity that shows the person is having a sensory experience, and the person's mind has the sensory experiences.

Physicists suggest that another process must be occurring, such as sound pulses. But as of yet, they have no indication that is true.

Evidence Demonstrating That Your Mind Is Not in Your Brain Proves You Will Never Die

Neuroscientists cannot find the mind in the brain or explain how a brain could create a mind; remote viewers have sense experiences of things far removed from them; people with parts of their brain removed or with little brain tissue live perfectly normal lives; people having NDEs and OBEs have full sensory experiences of distant places when the body and brain are incapacitated; and no electrical signal can be detected between sensory organs and the brain. These facts lead to the conclusion that the mind is independent of the brain. Thus, when the brain dies, the mind that is outside of the brain continues living unaffected by the demise of the brain.

The fact that your mind is not in your brain and is unaffected by the brain's death proves you will never die.

Chapter 14

Evidence from Near-Death Experiences Demonstrates You Will Live After Your Body Dies

Today medical science is able to revive people whose bodies show little or no brain function. When they come back from the brink of death, many share remarkable accounts of feelings of calm and peace, moving upwards through a tunnel, meeting deceased loved ones, encountering a being of light, experiencing a life review, feeling unconditionally loved, being given a choice to stay or return, and feeling a return to the body, often very reluctantly. They have had a near-death experience (NDE).

During the NDE, the body and brain have lost mental and physical vitality—they are dying. Although during the NDE the brain is not capable of experiencing higher functions that neuroscience associates with awareness, such as sensory experiences, judgment, and memory, experiencers report that their senses are more acute than normal, with vivid visual experiences and feelings of physical comfort and lightness and no pain, even when the body is in trauma. Rather than feeling the fear and dread one would expect during life-ending traumatic experiences, people feel profound peace. They are on the bluff at the end of this life, enthralled by the vista before them of indescribable beauty, peacefulness, and unconditional love.

1. More Acute Senses When They Should Be Failing

Dr. Jeffrey Long, founder of the Near-Death Research Foundation, explains that trauma to the dying brain and body should cause a brain to lose capabilities, resulting in confusion and cessation of awareness and memory. But that is not what happens.

> Research says that memories formed just before or after a period of cardiac arrest, if they occur at all, are marked by confusion. By contrast, NDEs contain confused memories only rarely. If any part of the NDE were due to simple reconstruction of memory fragments, such memories would be expected to become progressively more or less confused as the NDEer approached or recovered from unconsciousness. This is not what happens. Near death experiences are typically highly lucid from beginning to end... We have found that the highest level of consciousness and alertness is usually experienced not at the beginning or end of the NDE but somewhere during or throughout the entire NDE.... In addition, NDE research shows people in and out of body state usually experience a higher level of consciousness and alertness than they experience on a day-to-day basis during their everyday lives.[152]

Dr. Peter Fenwick, a neuropsychiatrist and one of the leading authorities in Britain on NDEs, explains that the condition of the brain during NDEs should result in confusion and paranoia, but it doesn't.

> Paradox cerebral localization studies have indicated that complex subjective experiences are mediated through the activation of a number of different cortical areas, rather than any single area of the brain. A globally disordered brain would not be expected to support lucid thought

processes or the ability to "see," "hear," and remember details of the experience. Any acute alteration in cerebral physiology leads to confusion and impaired higher cerebral function.... Cerebral damage, particularly hippocampal damage, is common after cardiac arrest; thus only confusional and paranoid thinking as is found in intensive care patients should occur. The paradox is that experiences reported by cardiac arrest patients are not confusional. On the contrary, they indicate heightened awareness, attention, and memory at a time when consciousness and memory formation are not expected to be functioning.[153]

During the NDE, no sensory experiences and no memory production would be possible if the mind were located in the brain. During these times, people whose brain activity is being monitored are showing absolutely no life in the brain. Dr. Fenwick describes the state of the brain during an NDE:

The brain isn't functioning. It's not there. It's destroyed. It's abnormal. But, yet, it can produce these very clear experiences.... An unconscious state is when the brain ceases to function. For example, if you faint, you fall to the floor, you don't know what's happening and the brain isn't working. The memory systems are particularly sensitive to unconsciousness. So, you won't remember anything. But yet, after one of these experiences [an NDE], you come out with clear, lucid memories.... This is a real puzzle for science. I have not yet seen any good scientific explanation which can explain that fact.[154]

Researchers from the Copenhagen University Hospital found in their study of 289 NDEers that 65 percent reported having exceptional speed of thought, 63 percent reported having exceptionally vivid senses, and 53 percent felt separated from or out of their bodies.[155] As the body no longer impedes consciousness, all the faculties associated with the mind outside of the brain vitalize.

Another study, published in the journal *Resuscitation*, concluded that people with no brain function who describe an NDE in fact have lucid thought processes, reasoning, and memory during the period when their brains are not functioning. In the study performed by Dr. Sam Parnia and a colleague from Southampton General Hospital in England, the researchers interviewed 63 heart attack patients who had been evaluated to be clinically dead, but were subsequently resuscitated. To ensure that their recollections were fresh, the people were interviewed within a week of the experience. They described details and events in which they were thinking, reasoning, and consciously moving around during the period when they were unconscious, their bodies were motionless, and doctors working on them had determined their brains were not functioning.[156]

> When the brain is deprived of oxygen people become totally confused, thrash around and usually have no memories at all, Parnia said. ``Here you have a severe insult to the brain but perfect memory."
>
> Skeptics have also suggested that patients' memories occurred in the moments they were leaving or returning to consciousness. But Parnia said when a brain is traumatized by a seizure or car wreck a patient generally does not remember moments just before or after losing consciousness.
>
> Rather, there is usually a memory lapse of hours or days. "Talk to them. They'll tell you something like: 'I just remember seeing the car and the next thing I knew I was in the hospital,'" he said.

"With cardiac arrest, the insult to the brain is so severe it stops the brain completely. Therefore, I would expect profound memory loss before and after the incident," he added.

Since the initial experiment, Parnia and his colleagues have found more than 3,500 people with lucid memories that apparently occurred at times they were thought to be clinically dead. Many of the patients, he said, were reluctant to share their experiences fearing they would be thought crazy.[157]

A famous NDE demonstrating that people are having sensory experiences when the body's senses are blocked or not functioning was reported in *Light and Death*, a book by cardiologist Dr. Michael Sabom.[158] To remove a large, deadly aneurysm from beneath her brain, doctors put Pam Reynolds into a state of hypothermic cardiac arrest. Her body temperature was lowered to 60 degrees, her heartbeat and breathing were stopped, and the blood was drained from her head; her brain waves flattened, showing no brain activity. After her successful operation, she was warmed and her own blood was returned to her body. When she could communicate, she reported a startling NDE.

Reynolds gave remarkably accurate, detailed descriptions of the surgical procedure. She reported that someone in the operating room said something about her arteries being small, and she described the Midas Rex bone saw as looking like an electric toothbrush, having interchangeable blades and a high-pitched whirring sound.

The things she saw and heard occurred when she was deeply unconscious. During the time she described hearing and seeing details, her eyes were taped shut and her ears were plugged with devices that monitored her brain stem activity. These devices produced loud clicks measuring 95 decibels at a rate of 11.3 clicks per second, drowning out all outside noise.[159]

Reynolds reported floating out of the operating room and traveling down a tunnel to a light, at the end of which her deceased relatives and friends were waiting. Her long-dead grandmother was there. Eventually, her deceased uncle took her back and she reentered her body.

She said that during the experience she saw with vision that was "brighter and more focused and clearer than normal vision." When she heard her deceased grandmother calling, the sound was clearer than sounds she'd heard with her ears—yet her auditory functions were shut down by the noisy clicks and she was unconscious.

Five eminent cardiac and medical specialists (Sam Parnia, Pim Van Lommel, Robert Spetzler, Peter Fenwick, and Michael Sabom) all supported the accuracy of Reynolds's stated experience during her clinical death: "What she saw corresponded to what actually happened."[160] She had seen and heard details while either sensory deprived and unconscious, with her eyes taped shut and hearing blocked by loud clicks, or while she was brain dead.

2. Knowledge about Distant People and Events When Bodies and Brains Have No Access

Other evidence that in the NDE a person is moving into another realm is demonstrated by their knowledge about people and events distant from them. Their minds are freed from the body and use their heightened sense of awareness and perfectly functioning memory to observe and remember things happening distant from their unconscious bodies. Reports demonstrate that their minds are alive and acutely aware when their bodies have shut down.

Pediatrician Melvin Morse resuscitated a young girl named Katie who had nearly drowned after being under water for nineteen minutes. As a result of the massive swelling of the brain, fixed and dilated pupils, and breathing only with the assistance of an artificial lung, she had only a 10 percent chance of surviving. Against the odds, three days later she recovered fully. In the follow-up exam, Katie described many details of the emergency room and resuscitation although, during the entire ordeal, she was "profoundly comatose during, with her eyes closed." More importantly, Katie could recall many details far beyond the hospital. In one glimpse inside her own home, she described her mother preparing roast chicken and rice for dinner, where her father was sitting, what he was doing, and the specific toys her brother and sister were playing with. When Morse checked the details, the family confirmed that these events had occurred just days before.[161]

A young child's account is especially evidential of the separateness of mind and body because a naïve child reports what happens matter-of-factly. A five-year-old boy named Rick suffered from meningitis and fell into a coma. He was rushed to the hospital in an ambulance. Because of his near-death condition, Rick was outside of the body. As his body was taken away, he decided to stay behind. He watched family members' grief-stricken reactions to his emergency. He watched his father weeping as he entered the car to take the family to the hospital. Then he rushed to the hospital, arriving ahead of the ambulance, and watched hospital personnel move a girl about twelve years old out of the room he was to occupy.

Rick remained comatose for several days. When he was revived, he described all the events of the trauma and his family's behavior in perfect detail. His family was bewildered by the depth of his knowledge. He had been completely unconscious through it all.[162]

Evidence from Near-Death Experiences

Dr. Larry Dossey, former chief of staff of Medical City Dallas Hospital, describes this case of a woman blind from birth who is able to see clearly during her near-death experience:

> The surgery had gone smoothly until the late stages of the operation. Then something happened. As her physician was closing the incision, Sarah's heart stopped beating....
> [When she awoke, Sarah had] a clear, detailed memory of the frantic conversation of the surgeons and nurses during her cardiac arrest; the [operating room] layout; the scribbles on the surgery schedule board in the hall outside; the color of the sheets covering the operating table; the hairstyle of the head scrub nurse; the names of the surgeons in the doctors' lounge down the corridor who were waiting for her case to be concluded; and even the trivial fact that her anesthesiologist that day was wearing unmatched socks. All this she knew even though she had been fully anesthetized and unconscious during the surgery and the cardiac arrest.
>
> But what made Sarah's vision even more momentous was the fact that, since birth, she had been blind.[163]

Sarah's mind was able to see when her body couldn't because she was unconscious and had been blind since birth.

View the video of a woman who had been blind from birth, but was able to see during her near-death experience: www.earthschoolanswers.com/vicki/.

3. Knowledge That Is Not Understood but Later Validated

People having NDEs can learn things they don't understand until years later. During one NDE a patient saw his deceased grandmother. Beside her was a man he didn't recognize but who looked at him with love. More than ten years later he learned that he had been born out of wedlock during WWII. He was shown a photo of his biological father and recognized him as the man he had seen during his NDE. His father was Jewish and had been deported and killed.[164]

Experiencers sometimes learn information about deceased loved ones that they could only learn from them while in the NDE. Bruce Greyson, formerly a professor of psychiatry at the University of Connecticut, now Bonner-Lowry Professor of Personality Studies in the Department of Psychiatric Medicine at the University of Virginia in Charlottesville, described the following case.

> The author Maggie Callanan in her 1993 book, *Final Gifts*, wrote about an elderly Chinese woman who had an NDE in which she saw her deceased husband and her sister. She was puzzled since her sister wasn't dead, or so she thought. In actuality, her family had hid her sister's recent death from her for fear of upsetting her already fragile health.[165]

4. Feelings of Peace and Love Rather than Fear and Trauma

When the body and brain cease to function, the person having an NDE feels a profound sense of peace and love, not the fear and alarm that would be expected during trauma when life is slipping away. The experiencers are acutely aware and assess the situation and their prospects for the future with understanding. Rather than being dismayed and frightened by the prospect of leaving their bodies behind, they are profoundly peaceful, with a feeling of being so unconditionally loved that they don't want to return to the body.

[Jeffrey] Long found that many who survive these close calls with death report feelings of extraordinary peace and calm, as did a survivor of two cardiac arrests, who described how, "On the other side, the arms of my loved ones welcomed me home. The intense love just can't be described in words ... I felt content and safe, like I was in the care and love of God. And that love of God felt like the first time you see your baby or the first time you fall in love—multiplied by 10,000."[166]

The fact that people whose bodies and brains are clinically dead report feelings of peace rather than fear is evidence that as consciousness is freed from the body, it enters a realm characterized by peace and love, described as the life after this life.

Evidence from Near-Death Experiences Proves You Will Never Die

When the body is shutting down during an NDE, we should expect that the senses and memory will be impaired or nonexistent. Instead, the senses are more acute than normal and memory functions perfectly. We would also expect that the person with such acute senses would be fearful and traumatized by their bodily death. Instead, they are calm, with no pain or trauma, and feeling such an unconditional love they do not want to return to the body.

These experiences that are contrary to what we would expect when the brain and body are shutting down prove that when your brain and body die, you will not die.

Chapter 15

Highly Regarded Professionals Studying the Survival of Consciousness Have Concluded You Will Never Die

A great number of highly regarded, skeptical, logical researchers, scientists, and other scholars studied extensively and with an open mind the evidence for survival of consciousness after bodily death and became convinced of the reality of the survival of consciousness. Most began as skeptics with the goal of debunking mediums, which makes their testimonies and conclusions especially credible. This chapter lists some of them. There are many others who have come to the same conclusion.

1. Physicians Acknowledge Life after This Life

In a survey of 10,044 doctors in the U.S., 76 percent said they believe in God and 59 percent said they believe in some sort of afterlife. The doctors in the survey included Jewish, Hindu, Muslim, and Christian.[167]

2. Physical Scientists Who Have Studied Mediums Conclude Afterlife Communication Is Valid

Ron D. Pearson – British scientist, university lecturer, and engineer in thermodynamics and fluid mechanics who developed the theory of Survival Physics: "Survival of death is a natural fact of physics and efforts to discredit evidence of survival after death are in error."[168]

Jan Vandersande – Physicist, holder of three patents on thermoelectric materials, consultant to NASA, manager at the Jet Propulsion Laboratory, professor at Cornell University, and president and CEO of Mountain Province Diamonds. After investigating for over eight years materializations of those appearing from the life after this life, he became convinced that the materializations are people from the life after this life and that the life after this life is a reality.[169]

Thomas Alva Edison – Inventor of the phonograph and electric light bulb. Edison was a Spiritualist and experimented with mechanical means of contacting the dead.[170]

Sir Joseph John Thompson – Discoverer of the electron, professor of experimental physics at Cambridge, and winner of the 1906 Nobel Prize in physics. Thompson asserted that people continue to live after the body dies.[171]

Abdus Salam – Nobel laureate and director of the International Centre for Theoretical Physics. Salam studied the results of investigations of the evidence of the life after this life, concluding the life after this life is a reality.[172]

Sam Nicholls – Researcher into subatomic phenomena. Nicholls came to believe that people in the life after this life are composed of slightly different atomic components and that they exist in and share the same space with people on the earth plane.[173]

Augustus De Morgan – Considered one of the most brilliant mathematicians of the 19th century. De Morgan wrote about his first-hand experiences with mediums and that he was satisfied that the physical mediumship phenomena he witnessed was real.[174]

Robert Hare – Emeritus professor of chemistry at the University of Pennsylvania and world-renowned inventor. Hare set out to prove that the messages from the dead were either hallucinations or unconscious muscular actions on the part of those present. After extensive, critical study, he concluded the communications with his parents, sister, brother, and dearest friends were real.[175]

James J. Mapes – Professor of chemistry and natural philosophy at the National Academy of Design in New York and later at the American Institute. Mapes investigated many mediums in an effort to debunk them. He changed his views and both his wife and daughter became mediums. He concluded his study by writing that "spirits can and do communicate with mortals, and in all cases evince a desire to elevate and advance those they commune with."[176]

Allan Kardec – Professor of chemistry, physics, comparative anatomy, and astronomy. After thoroughly studying many mediums, Kardec concluded "that communication could be received through speech, hearing, sight, touch, etc., and even through direct writing of the spirits themselves – that is to say without the help of the medium's hand or of the pencil."[177]

Alfred Russel Wallace – Co-originator with Charles Darwin of the natural selection theory of evolution, and a naturalist who provided Darwin with his parallel theory, including the "survival of the fittest," before Darwin went public with their two theories. Wallace was a hard-core materialist until he began investigating mediums. He soon became one of the greatest proponents of the life after this life.[178]

Sir William Crookes – Physicist and chemist who discovered the element thallium, pioneer in radioactivity, and inventor of the radiometer, the spinthariscope, and a high-vacuum tube that contributed to the discovery of the x-ray. Crookes set out to "drive the worthless residuum of spiritualism" into the "unknown limbo of magic and necromancy." However, after thorough investigations of mediums, he wrote that the phenomena in séances "point to the existence of another order of human life continuous with this and demonstrate the possibility in certain circumstances of communication between this world and the next."[179]

Sir William Barrett – Professor of physics at the Royal College of Science in Dublin for thirty-seven years, discovering a silicon-iron alloy important to the development of the telephone and in the construction of transformers. Barrett was knighted in 1912 for his contributions to science. His study of the life after this life led him to conclude, "I am personally convinced that the evidence we have published decidedly demonstrates (1) the existence of a spiritual world, (2) survival after death, and (3) of occasional communication from those who have passed over."[180]

Sir Oliver Lodge – Professor of physics at University College in Liverpool, principal at the University of Birmingham, and pioneer in electricity, the radio, and the spark plug. Lodge was knighted in 1902 for his contributions to science. After studying extensively the séances of Leonora Piper and Gladys Osborne Leonard, he concluded, "People [in the life after this life] still continue to take an interest in what is going on, that they know far more about things on this earth than we do, and are able from time to time to communicate with us.... I do not say it is easy, but it is possible, and I have conversed with my friends just as I can converse with anyone in this audience now."[181]

Camille Flammarion – World-renowned astronomer, founder of the French Astronomical Society, known for his study of Mars, and pioneer in the use of balloons to study the stars. Flammarion investigated psychic phenomena, including mediumship, for more than fifty years and concluded, "I do not hesitate to affirm my conviction, based on personal examination of the subject, that any man who declares the phenomena to be impossible is one who speaks without knowing what he is talking about."[182]

Charles Richet – Professor of physiology at the University of Paris Medical School, world authority on nutrition in health and disease, and winner of the Nobel Prize in 1913 for his work on allergic reactions. While convinced of the reality of mediumship, Richet remained publicly agnostic toward the afterlife. According to Sir Oliver Lodge, his good friend, Richet accepted it before his death. He wrote, "It seems to me the facts are undeniable. I am convinced that I have been present at realities [medium sessions]."[183]

Robert Crookall – Lecturer at Aberdeen University before joining the staff of the British Geological Survey and specializing in coal-forming plants. Crookall's research into the life after this life was so compelling to him that he resigned from his geology work in 1952 to devote the rest of his life to psychical research. He wrote, "There is no longer a 'deadlock' or 'stalemate' on the question of survival. On the contrary, survival is as well established as the theory of evolution."[184]

Raynor C. Johnson – Physicist; Oxford scholar with a doctorate from the University of London; lecturer in physics at King's College, University of London; and master of Queen's College at the University of Melbourne. Johnson studied survival in depth to judge whether it was true. He concluded that "if survival of death is not rigorously proven, it is nevertheless established as of that high order or probability which, for practical purposes, can be taken as the same thing."[185]

John Logie Baird – Inventor of the television and infra-red camera. Baird stated that he had contacted the deceased Thomas

A. Edison through a medium. He confirmed the contact: "I have witnessed some very startling phenomena under circumstances which make trickery out of the question."[186]

George Meek – Scientist, inventor, designer, and manufacturer of devices for air conditioning and wastewater treatment. Meek referred to himself as a "natural skeptic" who felt that talk of a life after this life just didn't make sense. To study the concept he traveled the world interviewing top medical doctors, psychiatrists, physicists, biochemists, psychics, healers, parapsychologists, hypnotherapists, ministers, priests, and rabbis. He concluded that people are immortal and wrote his findings in his book *After We Die, What Then?*[187]

Archie Roy – Professor emeritus of Astronomy at the University of Glasgow; fellow of the Royal Society of Edinburgh, the Royal Astronomical Society, and the British Interplanetary Society; and head of the Advanced Scientific Institutes for NATO. After extensive study of psychic and medium activity, he wrote, "I am convinced now of the reality of such [psychic] phenomena.[188]

A. P. Hale – Physicist and electronics engineer. Hale conducted careful tests of electronic recordings of voices coming from the life after this life. He concluded, "In view of the tests carried out in a screened laboratory at my firm, I cannot explain what happened in normal physical terms."[189]

Sir Robert Mayer – Businessman and patron of music. After studying electronic recordings of voices coming from the life after this life, Mayer concluded, "If the experts are baffled, I consider this is a good enough reason for presenting the Voice Phenomena to the general public."[190]

3. Psychologists and Psychotherapists Have Concluded Afterlife Communication Is Valid

Psychologists and psychotherapists, who care for people in times of crisis, often hear accounts from patients of psychic activity and the life after this life; many have themselves had such experiences. They may not feel comfortable talking about the experiences because of the criticism they fear they would receive from colleagues. But when they're given the opportunity to speak about them in a safe group, the stories abound.

Dr. Elisabeth Lloyd Mayer, a professor of psychology at the University of California, Berkeley, and instructor at the University of California Medical Center studied and spoke about clairvoyance, was a psychoanalyst, researcher, clinician, and author of groundbreaking papers on female development, the nature of science, and intuition. Dr. Mayer wrote about the common reaction from medical and psychoanalytic professionals when she spoke about her own psychic experiences.

> As word of my new interest [in psychic events] spread, my medical and psychoanalytic colleagues began to inundate me with accounts of their own anomalous experiences, personal as well as clinical.... the stories they shared with me were often ones they'd never revealed to another professional associate. Their accounts—by email, snail mail, at conferences, in seminars, in hall corridors, or at dinner—made as little sense to me as they did to the colleagues telling me about them. The stories were all about knowing things in bizarrely inexplicable ways.... I was particularly fascinated by how eagerly my colleagues shared even the most weirdly personal stories with me. Their eagerness puzzled me, until I realized how badly people wanted to reintegrate corners of experience they'd walled off from their public lives for fear of being misbelieved.[191]

The same reluctance to speak about their experiences but having a great desire to do so is true for healthcare professionals who have seen evidence of the life after this life in their own lives and their patients' lives. However, afterlife communication experiences are common.

Dr. William James – One of America's foremost psychologists; wrote widely in psychology, philosophy, and religion while teaching at Harvard for thirty-five years; his *Principles of Psychology* (1890) became the seminal work in his field; also wrote the classic *Varieties of Religious Experience*. After investigating life after this life by sitting with medium Leonora Piper, James concluded, "One who takes part in a good sitting has usually a far livelier sense, both of the reality and of the importance of the communication, than one who merely reads the records."[192]

Dr. Allan Botkin – Clinical psychologist who discovered induced after-death communication (IADC) in 1995, now used by hundreds of psychotherapists, wrote, "I cannot imagine that if the afterlife is a reality, IADCs, ADCs, and NDEs are hallucinatory aberrations produced by our brains that lead us into misunderstanding."[193]

Dr. Cesare Lombroso – Professor of psychology at the University of Turin, inspector of asylums for the insane in Italy, and pioneering criminologist known worldwide for his book *The Criminal Man*.[194] He began investigating psychic phenomena in 1891 and as a result of his study concluded, "There can be no doubt that genuine psychical phenomena are produced by intelligences totally independent of the psychic and the parties present at the sittings."[195]

Dr. Bruce Greyson – Professor of psychiatry at the University of Connecticut, Chester F. Carlson Professor Emeritus of Psychiatry and Neurobehavioral Sciences at the University of Virginia, and near-death experience researcher for over twenty-five years. Greyson has written countless articles on the subject for the *Journal of Scientific Exploration, Journal of the American Medical Association, American Journal of Psychiatry,* and other leading science and medical publications. He concluded that "the survival hypothesis is the most parsimonious explanation for the growing database of near-death experiences."[196]

Dr. Julian Ochorowicz – Professor of psychology and philosophy at the University of Warsaw. Ochorowicz helped establish the Polish Psychological Institute in Warsaw and served as director for the International Institute of Psychology in Paris.[197]

Baron (Dr.) Albert Von Schrenck-Notzing – A forensic psychiatrist and member of the German aristocracy. Schrenck-Notzing collaborated with Richet, Lombroso, Lodge, and others in many investigations for over thirty years.[198]

Dr. Carl A. Wickland – Member of the Chicago Medical Society and American Association for the Advancement of Science, and director of the National Psychological Institute of Los Angeles, specializing in schizophrenia, paranoia, depression, addiction, manic-depression, criminal behavior, and phobias. Wickland's direct experiences led him to conclude that spirits on the next planes of life communicate with and affect people on the earth plane.[199]

Dr. Gardner Murphy – Hodgson Memorial Fund research grant recipient at Harvard, president of the American Society for Psychical Research for twenty years, assistant psychology professor at Columbia University, and chairman of the psychology department at City College of New York. After studying medium session records, Murphy wrote, "It is the autonomy, the purposiveness, the cogency, above all the individuality, of the [séance] sources of the messages, that cannot be by-passed.... The case looks like communication with the deceased."[200]

Dr. Gary Schwartz – PhD from Harvard University, professor of psychology and psychiatry at Yale University, and director of the Laboratory for Advances in Consciousness and Health at the University of Arizona. Schwartz conducted extensive research with mediums, detailed in his book *The Afterlife Experiments*.[201] He concluded, "I can no longer ignore the data [on research into the survival of consciousness] and dismiss the words [coming through mediums]. They are as real as the sun, the trees, and our television sets, which seem to pull pictures out of the air."[202]

Dr. Jon Klimo – Psychology professor for over thirty years, most recently at the American School of Professional Psychology, Argosy University. Klimo has done extensive research, writing, teaching, and presentations in psychology, parapsychology, consciousness studies, new paradigm thought, metaphysics, and the transpersonal domain. He concluded, "I personally choose to believe that we do meaningfully survive death and can communicate back through mediums and channels."[203]

Dr. David Fontana – Professor of transpersonal psychology in Great Britain, past president of the Society for Psychical Research, and fellow of the British Psychological Society. Dr. Fontana has done extensive survival research and is the author of many books, including *Is There an Afterlife?*[204] He wrote, "If your answer [to questions of our existence] is that you are more than a biological accident whose ultimately meaningless life is bounded by the cradle and the grave, then I have to say I agree with you."[205]

Dr. Brendan Rooney – Director of the Institute of Psychology in Dublin. After investigating electronic voice recordings of the deceased speaking to the living, Rooney concluded, "I have apparently succeeded in reproducing the phenomena. Voices have appeared on a tape which did not come from any known source."[206]

Carl G. Jung – Eminent psychoanalyst, contemporary of Freud, and father of Jungian psychology. Jung wrote after his own NDE, "What happens after death is so unspeakably glorious, that our imagination and feelings do not suffice to form even an approximate conception of it."[207]

One Hundred Well-Known Scientists – These scientists, all profoundly skeptical and some openly hostile, declared themselves, without exception, completely convinced after having worked under the direction of Dr. Schrenck-Notzing with his medium Willy Schneider.[208]

4. Professors of the Humanities Studying Afterlife Communication Have Concluded It Is Valid

Frederic W. H. Myers – English poet, critic, and essayist; fellow, classical lecturer, and school inspector at Trinity College, Cambridge; and co-founder of the Society for Psychical Research, London. After studying mediums and the life after this life, Myers concluded, "messages of the departing and the departed, have, to my mind actually proved: a) In the first place, they prove survival pure and simple; the persistence of the spirit's life as a structural law of the universe; the inalienable heritage of each several soul."[209]

Dr. Richard Hodgson – MA and LLD from the University of Melbourne, poetry and philosophy instructor at University Extension, and instructor of the philosophy of Herbert Spenser at Cambridge. Hodgson and William James decided to witness a number of séances to, as he wrote, "discover fraud and trickery." After hundreds of sittings with medium Leonora Piper over eighteen years, he concluded, "The truth has been given to me in such a way as to remove from me the possibility of a doubt [of the continuance of life after death]."[210]

Dr. James H. Hyslop – PhD from Johns Hopkins University; LLD from University of Wooster; philosophy teacher at Lake Forest University, Smith College, and Bucknell University;

professor at Columbia University. Hyslop wrote three textbooks: *Elements of Logic* (1892), *Elements of Ethics* (1895), and *Problems of Philosophy* (1905). His research brought him to conclude, "Personally, I regard the fact of survival after death as scientifically proved."[211]

Dr. Hamlin Garland – Pulitzer Prize-winning author of fifty-two books. Garland was intimately involved with major literary, social, and artistic movements in American culture. His experiences in séances convinced him of the survival of consciousness.[212]

Maurice Maeterlinck – Nobel laureate in literature; poet, author, and playwright; and psychic researcher. Based on his research he concluded that there is no "trickery" in afterlife communication in séances. The experiences are genuine.[213]

Dr. William R. Newbold – Professor of philosophy at the University of Pennsylvania, where he was a member of the advisory council of the American Society for Psychical Research. Newbold had numerous sittings with medium Leonora Piper. He concluded that the evidence in medium experiences of "the essential independence of the mind and the body, of the existence of a supersensible world, and of the possibility of occasional communication between that world and this… [is] evidence that is worthy of consideration for all these points."[214]

Dr. C. J. Ducasse – Chairman of the Department of Philosophy at Brown University. A French-born American philosopher, Ducasse came to the United States as a teenager. He had many sittings with mediums and lectured extensively on psychical research. He concluded the following:

> The belief in life after death, which so many persons have found no particular difficulty in accepting as an article in religious faith, may well be capable of empirical proof. That the occurrence of paranormal phenomena does appear to have

such implications is, I submit, sufficient reason to give them far more attention and study than they have commonly received in the past.[215]

Dr. Hornell Hart – Professor of Sociology at Duke University and author of several important books on social and psychological problems. Hart reviewed the literature on the life after this life and concluded, "Human personality does survive bodily death."[216]

Colin Brookes-Smith – British engineer. Brookes-Smith joined a group to study the life after this life and psychic phenomena. As a result of his experiences, he stated in the *Journal of the Society for Psychical Research* that survival should be regarded as a sufficiently well-established fact to be beyond denial by any reasonable person. He described it as "a momentous scientific conclusion of prime importance to mankind."[217]

Arthur Balfour – Prime Minister of the United Kingdom from 1902 to 1905, Secretary of State, and author of *A Defense of Philosophic Doubt.*[218] Balfour studied the life after this life and mediums and felt sufficiently convinced to write elaborately about them in the *Proceedings of the Society for Psychical Research*.

5. Attorneys Who Have Studied Afterlife Communication Have Concluded It Is Valid

Attorneys are trained in analyzing testimonies and data from witnesses. Those who carefully analyze the activities of mediums certify that mediums are communicating with people living in the life after this life. Attorneys who review the evidence for the life after this life are convinced of its reality.

Edward C. Randall – Prominent Buffalo, New York, trial lawyer; member of the board of directors of a number of large corporations. Randall had more than seven hundred sittings with direct-voice medium Emily S. French over twenty-two years. He wrote, "Hundreds, yea thousands [of spirits], have come and talked with me, and to many whom I have invited to participate in the work – thousands of different voices with different tones, different thoughts, different personalities, no two alike; and at times in different languages."[219]

Victor James Zammit – Retired lawyer of the Supreme Court of New South Wales and the High Court of Australia. Zammit's extensive education includes a BA in psychology, a graduate degree in education, an MA in legal history, a Bachelor of Laws, and a PhD in law. After examining the evidence for the life after this life, he wrote, "After many years of serious investigation, I have come to the irretrievable conclusion that there is a great body of evidence which, taken as a whole, absolutely and unqualifiedly proves the case for the afterlife."[220]

John Worth Edmonds – Circuit judge, state Supreme Court judge, member of the New York assembly, and colonel in the militia. Confused about death and the life after this life, and with no confidence in either the church or mediums, Edmonds launched an investigation into the activities of mediums. He visited a variety of mediums and evaluated their sessions using various devices. As a result, he wrote that "the phenomena were not produced by any person in the rooms."[221]

William Dean Shuart – Surrogate judge of Monroe County, New York. Shuart attended the same circles as Edward C. Randall did, conducted a variety of "exacting experiments," and became equally convinced of their reality and validity.[222]

Aubrey Rose, OBE, CBE – British human rights lawyer. After empirically investigating transmissions made by one of his colleagues through direct voice medium Leslie Flint, Rose stated that without doubt the voice he heard in a session came from the life after this life and was that of Judge Lord Birkett, who had crossed over some time before.[223]

6. Clergy Who Have Studied Afterlife Communication Have Concluded It Is Possible and Valid

Members of the clergy have an especially difficult time in voicing their convictions about the life after this life described by mediums because of the narrow views of most religions. But those who do study the imminent life after this life become convinced of its reality as the mediums describe it, not as religion teaches it.

Isaac K. Funk – Lutheran minister, co-founder of Funk and Wagnalls, and editor-in-chief of the *Standard Dictionary of the English Language*. After his studies, Funk wrote, "I have the absolute assurance that when the something we call death comes, it will only mean a new and larger and more complete life."[224]

Charles Drayton Thomas – Graduate of Richmond Theological College and Methodist minister. Thomas served on the Council of the Society for Psychical Research in London for nineteen years. Beginning in 1917, he had more than five hundred sittings with Gladys Osborne Leonard, probably England's most famous medium. He concluded that there should be "a general acceptance of this evidence for survival."[225]

Pere Francois Brune – Catholic priest, member of the Catholic Institute in Paris and Biblical Institute in Rome, theologian, and professor in a number of leading seminaries. Brune wrote that the Catholic Church's attitude about communication from the life after this life is changing: "I believe that, as several of these messages assure us, we in fact are never alone. Some deceased, once they have arrived in the Beyond, appear to have the wish of continuing their life through us, and come to sponge on us."[226]

In another statement, Brune wrote about the changing position of the church on the life after this life:

> We do not have to do an official change of the Church's position. But it is in fact an evolution that without any

doubt is due to the realization that the phenomena exist, and that they—how complex they ever may be—indeed correspond very often to an authentic communication with our dead.[227]

Dr. Peter Bander – Senior lecturer in religious and moral education at the Cambridge Institute of Education. Bander is a psychologist and Christian theologian. He began his investigation of the life after this life stating clearly that it was impossible for dead people to communicate with the living, that it was not only far-fetched but outrageous to even think about. However, after participating in a study of electronic voice production (EVP), he concluded: "I noticed the peculiar rhythm mentioned by Raudive and his colleagues.... I heard a voice.... I believed this to have been the voice of my mother who had died three years earlier."[228]

7. Church Bodies Who Have Studied Mediums Have Concluded the Communications Are Valid

The Church of England

A committee of the Church of England studied mediumship records for two years, analyzing a great volume of the evidence on mediumship to investigate Spiritualism because it was so popular in England at the time. Its investigations included clergy sitting with some of the leading mediums in England. At the end of their thorough investigation, seven of the ten members of the committee—against enormous pressure—came to this conclusion: "The hypothesis that they (spirit communications) proceed in some cases from discarnate spirits is the true one."[229]

The Roman Catholic Church

The Rev. Gino Concetti, chief theological commentator for the Vatican newspaper, L'Osservatore Romano, wrote,

"Communication is possible between those who live on this earth and those who live in a state of eternal repose, in heaven or purgatory. It may even be that God lets our loved ones send us messages to guide us at certain moments in our life."[230]

Concetti suggested dead relatives could be responsible for prompting impulses, triggering inspiration, and appearing in dreams. He said the new Catholic catechism specifically endorses the view that the dead could intercede on earth and quotes the dying St. Dominic telling his brothers: "Do not weep, for I shall be more useful to you after my death and I shall help you then more effectively than during my life."[231]

8. Debunkers Who Have Studied Afterlife Communication Openly Conclude It Is Valid

Well-educated, highly regarded scholars determined to debunk mediums assert after their efforts that the mediums are communicating with people whose bodies have died.

Dr. Hereward Carrington – American psychic investigator and author. After moving to the U.S. from Great Britain in 1899, Carrington served as assistant to Dr. James H. Hyslop at the Society for Psychical Research. His first of many books on psychical phenomena was published in 1907 and explained the fraudulent practices of physical mediums. However, Carrington came away from his investigation of Italian physical medium Eusapia Palladino convinced of the reality of some of the phenomena.

> I myself have observed materializations under perfect conditions of control and have had the temporary hand melt within my own, as I held it firmly grasped. This hand was a perfectly formed physiological structure, warm, lifelike, and having all the attributes of the human hand – yet both the medium's hands were securely held by two controllers, and

visible in the red light. Let me repeat, this hand was not pulled away, but somehow melted in my grasp as I held it.[232]

Dr. Harry Price – British psychic researcher and author. A debunker of fraudulent mediums, Price came to believe in genuine psychic phenomena and founded the National Laboratory of Psychical Research, later the University of London Council for Psychical Research. About his research he wrote, "And if I were not convinced of these [medium phenomena], I would not waste another moment of my time or penny of my money in further research."[233]

Conclusion

Verified evidence from reliable sources proves beyond a reasonable doubt that human consciousness survives bodily death. Studies of consciousness and communication by people alive in the life after this life demonstrate that people communicating from the next life

- Comment on contemporary life activities validated by the people engaged in them, demonstrating that they are alive at the time preceding the communication and during the communication
- Have fully capable mental capacities showing no damage from the death of the brain
- Carry on fluid conversations with voice characteristics and knowledge that were characteristic of them when they lived on the earth plane
- Have personalities that are recognized by those experiencing the communication because of intimate relationships or knowledge about the person in spirit
- Recall and speak fluidly and accurately about details of their experiences during their lives before their body ceased to function that are validated by people who know them
- Sometimes have highly specialized knowledge that the medium could not know but that they and the person receiving the communication on earth understand
- Materialize, and those who knew them on earth testify that the materialization is clearly recognizable as the person

Those receiving communications from people in the life after this life

- Can be led into a state of mind in which they have life-changing communication.
- Can have visitations in dreams.

It is also true beyond a reasonable doubt that people survive bodily death because of the following:

- Afterlife communication experiences are common.
- Consciousness is fundamental. As individuated manifestations of the Universal Intelligence, we change from one state of being to another, but as the Universal Intelligence cannot die, so our consciousness cannot die.
- The functions commonly associated with consciousness have been shown to occur when the brain is not involved, so when the brain dies, consciousness is not affected.
- When people having near-death experiences are on the brink of bodily death, their senses become more acute, their mental functions are enhanced, their bodily issues such as pain disappear, they are pervaded by a sense of wellbeing rather than trauma and fear, and their memory functions perfectly. These phenomena demonstrate that as the body ceases to function, consciousness is enhanced—revealing its transition into the life after this life.

The Message for Humankind

Humankind has steadily evolved in wisdom by discovering new truths that replace erroneous beliefs long held to be true by highly regarded scholars. People came to realize the earth is not the center of the universe, bloodletting does not cure disease, plagues are not caused by vapors, and heavenly bodies are not revolving on concentric crystalline spheres.

In the same way, humankind has held erroneous beliefs about who we are in eternity, what happens at the transition from this life, and what our lives will be like after leaving this life. Today people are evolving to realize we are spiritual beings having a physical experience. Our Souls planned this time in earth school for us to learn lessons, grow in love and compassion, and enjoy this life. Humankind is also learning that when we have finished with what we set out to do, we will graduate in an easy, unremarkable transition into a wonderful new life where we will have reunions with all the people and pets we love.

Humankind is evolving to realize beyond a reasonable doubt that we survive the death of our bodies.

You will never die.

Endnotes

[1] Leslie Flint Educational Trust, 22B Brunswick Park, London SE5 7RJ, England, www.leslieflint.com.

[2] "Direct Voice: Conversation between mother and her deceased son," Man and the unknown, Michael Rogge, August 17, 1996, www.xs4all.nl/~wichm/fearon.html.

[3] Leslie Flint et al., *Chapters of Experience* (London: Muller, 1973), 11.

[4] Flint, *Chapters of Experience*.

[5] Leslie Flint, Douglas Conacher, and Eira Conacher, *There Is Life after Death: Tape Recordings from the Other World* (Ontario, Canada: Howard Baker Press, 1978).

[6] Flint, *Chapters of Experience*.

[7] G. Smith, *The Unbelievable Truth* (Carlsbad, CA: Hay House, 2004).

[8] Tim Woolworth, "Konstantin Raudive and His ITC EVP Breakthrough," ITC Voices, February 6, 2011, http://itcvoices.org/konstantin-raudive-and-his-itc-evp-breakthrough/.

[9] Stephen Braude, "The Mediumship of Carlos Mirabelli (1889-1951)," *Journal of Scientific Exploration* 31, no. 3 (September 2017): 435-456.

[10] Braude, "The Mediumship of Carlos Mirabelli," 435-456.

[11] "Mirabelli, Carlos Carmine," The Free Dictionary by Farlex, https://encyclopedia2.thefreedictionary.com/Mirabelli%2c+Carlos+Carmine.

[12] Eurico de Goes, *Prodígios da Biopsychica obtidos com o Médium Mirabelli* (São Paulo: Typographia Cupol, 1937), 129.

[13] Helen Duncan and C. E. Bechhofer Roberts, *The Trial of Mrs. Duncan* (London: Jarrolds Publishers, 1945), 171-172.

[14] Duncan, *The Trial of Mrs. Duncan*, 288-291.

[15] Duncan, *The Trial of Mrs. Duncan*, 257 – 260.

[16] Duncan, *The Trial of Mrs. Duncan*, 270-272.

[17] Duncan, *The Trial of Mrs. Duncan*, 295-296.

[18] "The Return of Montague [sic] Keen," Victor Zammit, https://victorzammit.com/MontagueKeentapes/Montague%20Keen%20-%20transcript16thApril2004.htm.

[19] Konstantin Raudive, *Breakthrough: An Amazing Experiment in Electronic Communication with the Dead*, (Colin Smythe Ltd, 1971).

[20] Carl Michael von Hausswolff, "Investigation Studio for Audioscopic Communications," *Cabinet Magazine*, Winter 200-2001, https://www.cabinetmagazine.org/issues/1/vonhausswolff.php.

[21] George W. Meek, et al. *Spiricom: An Electronic-Etheric Systems Approach to Communications with Other Levels of Human Consciousness* (Metascience Research, 1982).

[22] Elizabeth Kübler-Ross, *On Life after Death* (Berkeley, CA: Celestial Arts, 2008).

[23] Raymond Moody, "Family Reunions: Visionary Encounters with the Departed in a Modern-Day Psychomanteum," *Journal of Near-Death Studies* 11, no. 2 (Winter 1992): 112.

[24] Moody, "Family Reunions."

[25] J. B. Phillips, *Ring of Truth* (London: H. Shaw, 1977), 117.

[26] "A Theology of Ghosts," Thoughts of Loy, Loy Mershimer blogspot, September 19, 2005, http://loymershimer.blogspot.com/2005/09/theology-of-ghosts.html.

[27] Edmund Gurney et al., *Phantasms of the Living* (London: Trubner, 1886).

[28] Gurney, *Phantasms of the Living*.

[29] A. McKenzie, *Apparitions and Ghosts: A Modern Study* (London: Arthur Baker Ltd., 1971), 116-117.

[30] D. Scott Rogo, *Leaving the Body: A Complete Guide to Astral Projection* (New York: Fireside/Simon & Schuster, 1993), 16-17.

[31] A. Spraggett, *The Case for Immortality* (Scarborough, Canada: New American Library of Canada, 1974), 45-46.

[32] R. C. Johnson, *The Imprisoned Splendour* (Wheaton, IL: Quest Books, 1982), 198-199.

[33] E. Bennett, *Apparitions and Haunted Houses: A Survey of Evidence* (London: Faber and Faber, 1939), 131-132.

[34] Michael Tymn, "A veridical death-bed vision," Paranormal and Life After Death, March 14, 2008, https://paranormalandlifeafterdeath.blogspot.com/2008/03/.

³⁵ Allan L. Botkin and R. Craig Hogan, *Induced After-Death Communication: A Miraculous Therapy for Grief and Loss* (Charlottesville, VA: Hampton Roads Publishing, 2014), 12.

³⁶ Botkin, *Induced After-Death Communication*.

³⁷ Botkin, *Induced After-Death Communication*.

³⁸ Botkin, *Induced After-Death Communication*, 82-84.

³⁹ Botkin, *Induced After-Death Communication*, 84-85.

⁴⁰ Botkin, *Induced After-Death Communication*, 86-87.

⁴¹ Botkin, *Induced After-Death Communication*, 87-88.

⁴² Botkin, *Induced After-Death Communication*, 88-89.

⁴³ Rochelle Wright and R. Craig Hogan, *Repair & Reattachment Grief Therapy* (Chicago: Greater Reality Publications, 2015).

⁴⁴ Wright, *Repair & Reattachment*, 17-18.

⁴⁵ Jane Bissler, "Voices Across the Veil Direct Personal Communication," https://voicesacrosstheveil.afterlifedata.com/direct-personal-communication.

⁴⁶ Loving Hearts Connection session with Jane Bissler, September 14, 2021.

⁴⁷ Charles H. Hapgood, *Voices of Spirit* (New York: Delacorte Press/Seymour Lawrence, 1975).

⁴⁸ James H. Hyslop, *Life After Death: Problems of the Future Life and Its Nature* (Whitefish, MT: Kessinger Publishing, 1918).

⁴⁹ Ronan Crowley and Geert Lernout, "Joseph MacCabe in Ulysses," *Genetic Joyce Studies* 12 (Spring 2012).

⁵⁰ Richard Hodgson, "A further record of observations of certain phenomena of a trance," *Proceedings of the Society for Psychical Research* 13 (1897-1898): 297.

⁵¹ Michael Schmicker, *Best Evidence* (Lincoln, NE: Writers Club Press, 2002), 249-250.

⁵² Schmicker, *Best Evidence*, 251.

⁵³ Zammit, *A Lawyer Presents*, 119.

⁵⁴ Victor Zammit, *A Lawyer Presents the Case for the Afterlife* (Sydney, Australia: Ganmell Pty. Ltd., 2006): 116-117.

⁵⁵ Harry Price, *Leaves from a Psychist's Case-Book* (London: Victor Gollancz, 1933), Chapter VI.

⁵⁶ "Herbert Carmichael Irwin," This Day in Aviation, https://www.thisdayinaviation.com/tag/herbert-carmichael-irwin/.

⁵⁷ Schmicker, *Best Evidence*, 252-253.

⁵⁸ Sir Oliver Lodge, *Raymond or Life and Death* (New York: George H. Doran, 1916), 106.

⁵⁹ Lodge, *Raymond or Life and Death*, 106.

⁶⁰ Lodge, *Raymond or Life and Death*, 106-107.

⁶¹ Lodge, *Raymond or Life and Death*, 107-109.

⁶² Lodge, *Raymond or Life and Death*, 111-112.

⁶³ Lodge, *Raymond or Life and Death*, 140 and 152.

⁶⁴ Lodge, *Raymond or Life and Death*, 140 and 152.

⁶⁵ Lodge, *Raymond or Life and Death*, 260.

⁶⁶ Lodge, *Raymond or Life and Death*, 140 and 152.

⁶⁷ Jean Balfour, "The 'Palm Sunday' Case: New Light on an Old Love Story," *Proceedings of the Society for Psychical Research* 52 (1960): 79-267.

⁶⁸ Jill Galvan, "Tennyson's Ghosts: The Psychical Research Case of the Cross-Correspondences, 1901-c.1936," Branch Collective, https://www.branchcollective.org/?ps_articles=jill-galvan-tennysons-ghosts-the-psychical-research-case-of-the-cross-correspondences-1901-c-1936.

⁶⁹ Galvan, "Tennyson's Ghosts."

⁷⁰ Trevor Hamilton, "The Cross-Correspondences," Psi Encyclopedia, March 24, 2017, https://psi-encyclopedia.spr.ac.uk/articles/cross-correspondences.

⁷¹ Hamilton, "The Cross-Correspondences."

⁷² "Medium Alice Holland, England. UK.," Psychic Truth, http://psychictruth.info/Medium_Alice_Holland.htm.

⁷³ Zammit, *A Lawyer Presents*, 128.

⁷⁴ Colin Wilson, *Afterlife: An Investigation* (New York: Doubleday, 1987), 161.

⁷⁵ Gary Schwartz and W. L. Simon, *The Afterlife Experiments* (New York: Atria Books, 2003).

76 Gary Schwartz et al., "Accuracy and Replicability of Anomalous After-Death Communication Across Highly Skilled Mediums," *Journal of the Society for Psychical Research* 65 (2001): 1-25.

77 Schwartz, *The Afterlife Experiments*.

78 Julie Beischel and Gary Schwartz, "Anomalous information reception by research mediums demonstrated using a novel triple-blind protocol," *Explore* 3, no. 1 (January 2007): 23-27.

79 Kevin Williams, "Edgar Cayce on Dreams," June 28, 2020, online post, https://near-death.com/edgar-cayce-on-dreams/.

80 Botkin, *Induced After-Death Communication*.

81 Botkin, *Induced After-Death Communication*.

82 Wills-Brandon, *One Last Hug*.

83 Claudia Carlton Lambright, *Just a Dream Away: After-Death Communication through Dreams* (Self-published, December 7, 2020).

84 Lambright, *Just a Dream Away*, cited in Raymond Moody, "Dreams as Communication from the Afterlife," April 27, 2021, https://lifeafterlife.com/blog/dreams-as-communication-from-the-afterlife/.

85 Lambright, *Just a Dream Away*, cited in Moody.

86 Lawrence Vargas et al., "Exploring the multidimensional aspects of grief reactions," *American Journal of Psychiatry* 146, no. 11 (1989): 1484-9.

87 David Hay, "The spirituality of the unchurched," *Mission and Spirituality* (2002): 11-26.

88 Melvin Morse, "Near-death experiences and death-related visions in children: implications for the clinician," *Current Problems in Pediatrics* 24 (1994): 55-83.

89 W. Dewi Rees, "The hallucinations of widowhood," *British Medical Journal* (1971): 4, 37-41.

90 Jan Holden, "J. Holden describes the frequency of after-death communication," University of North Texas News Service, November 5, 2005.

91 Erlendur Haraldsson, "Survey of claimed encounters with the dead," *Omega* 19 (1989): 103-13.

92 Richard A. Kalish and David K. Reynolds, "Phenomenological reality and post death contact," *Journal for the Scientific Study of Religion* (1973): 209-21.

[93] William Matchett, "Repeated hallucinatory experiences as part of the mourning process among Hopi Indian women," Psychiatry 35, no. 2 (May 1972): 185-94.

[94] Bill Guggenheim and Judy Guggenheim, *Hello from Heaven* (New York: Bantam Books, 1995).

[95] Hans Holzer, *Ghost Hunter* (New York: Bobbs Merrill Company, 1963).

[96] C. A. Moore, "The unseen realm: Science is making room for near-death experiences beyond this world," *Desert Morning News*, February 18, 2006.

[97] Stephen Wagner, "Deathbed visions," Liveabout.com, January 2, 2019, http://paranormal.about.com/library/weekly/aa021901a.htm.

[98] Melvin Morse with Paul Perry, *Parting Visions* (New York: Villard Books, 1994).

[99] Diane Komp, *A Window to Heaven: When Children See Life in Death* (Grand Rapids, Michigan: Zondervan Publishing, 1992).

[100] Elisabeth Kübler-Ross, *On Children and Death* (New York: MacMillan Publishing, 1983).

[101] Karlis Osis and Erlendur Haraldsson, *At the Hour of Death* (Norwalk, CT: Hastings House, 1997).

[102] Osis, *At the Hour of Death*, 192.

[103] Carla Wills-Brandon, *One Last Hug Before I Go: The Mystery and Meaning of Deathbed Visions* (Norwalk, CT: Hastings House, 2007).

[104] Wills-Brandon, *One Last Hug*.

[105] Peter Fenwick, "Approaching-Death Experiences and the NDE: A Model for the Dying Process?" IANDS, June 24, 2017, https://www.iands.org/research/nde-research/important-research-articles/42-dr-peter-fenwick-md-science-and-spirituality.html?start=5.

[106] Anil Ananthaswamy, "What Does Quantum Theory Actually Tell Us about Reality?" *Scientific American Blog*, September 3, 2018. https://blogs.scientificamerican.com/observations/what-does-quantum-theory-actually-tell-us-about-reality/.

[107] Bruce Rosenblum and Fred Kuttner, *The Quantum Enigma* (Oxford: Oxford University Press, 2011), 81.

[108] Bernard Haisch, "Quantum Mechanics and Consciousness: A New Measurement" presentation, 27th Annual Society for Scientific Exploration Conference, Boulder, CO, 2008.

[109] Haisch, "Quantum Mechanics and Consciousness."

[110] Arjun Walia, "'Consciousness Creates Reality'—Physicists Admit the Universe Is Immaterial, Mental, & Spiritual," Transcend Media Service, April 20, 2015, citing R. C. Henry, "The Mental Universe," Nature 436, 2005: 29, quoting Sir James Jeans. https://www.transcend.org/tms/2015/04/consciousness-creates-reality-physicists-admit-the-universe-is-immaterial-mental-spiritual/.

[111] Adam Becker, *What Is Real?: The Unfinished Quest for the Meaning of Quantum Physics* (New York: Basic Books, 2018).

[112] Anil Ananthaswamy, "What Does Quantum Theory Actually Tell Us about Reality?" *Scientific American blogs,* September 3, 2018, https://blogs.scientificamerican.com/observations/what-does-quantum-theory-actually-tell-us-about-reality/.

[113] Andrew Truscott, "Experiment Confirms Quantum Theory Weirdness," press release, Australian National University, ScienceDaily, May 27, 2015, https://www.sciencedaily.com/releases/2015/05/150527103110.htm.

[114] R. Craig Hogan, *There Is Nothing but Mind and Experiences* (Normal, IL: Greater Reality Publications, 2020).

[115] Kenneth Ring and Sharon Cooper, *Mindsight: Near-Death and Out-of-Body Experiences in the Blind* (Bloomington, Indiana: iUniverse, 2008).

[116] Stephan Patt, "Brain localization of consciousness? Neurological considerations," lecture, 7th International Interdisciplinary Seminar, Exploring the Human Mind: The Perspective of Natural Sciences, Ponte di Legno, Italy, December 28, 2003.

[117] John Maddox, "The Unexpected Science to Come," *Scientific American* 281 (December 1999): 62-67.

[118] David E. Presti, "Book Review: Irreducible Mind: Toward a Psychology for the 21st Century," *Journal of Near-Death Studies* (Autumn 2008): 64.

[119] Stuart Hameroff, "Overview: Could life and consciousness be related to the fundamental quantum nature of the universe?" *Quantum Consciousness,* www.quantumconsciousness.org/content/overview-sh.

[120] David Chalmers, "The Puzzle of Conscious Experience," *Scientific American* 26, no. 3 (summer 1917), special issue "Mysteries of the mind."

[121] "Life After Death: Episode 8, The testimony of science," hosted by Tom Harpur, TV documentary, directed by Dan Robinson, aired 1996.

[122] Chris Carter, Rebuttal to Keith Augustine's attack of "Does Consciousness Depend on the Brain?" accessed May 30, 2007, www.survivalafterdeath.info/articles/carter/augustine.htm.

[123] Cyril Burt, *The Gifted Child* (New York: Wiley, 1975), 60.

[124] "Why Pioneer Neurosurgeon Wilder Penfield Said the Mind Is More than the Brain," interview of Michael Egnor by Robert J. Marks, Mind Matters News, podcast audio, February 29, 2020, https://mindmatters.ai/2020/02/why-pioneer-neurosurgeon-wilder-penfield-said-the-mind-is-more-than-the-brain.

[125] Sam Parnia et al., "Aware—Awareness during Resuscitation—A prospective study," *Resuscitation* 85, no. 12 (December 1, 2014): 1799-1805.

[126] Subhash Kak, Deepak Chopra, and Means Kafatos, "Perceived reality, quantum mechanics, and consciousness," *Cosmology* 18 (2014): 231-245.

[127] Tijn Touber, "Life goes on," *Ode* 3, no. 10 (December 2005).

[128] Victor Zammit, "Australian psychics beat 'orthodox' science,'" Victor Zammit, accessed May 13, 2007, http://victorzammit.com/articles/sensingmurder.html.

[129] "Psychic Detectives," transcript, CNN, "Nancy Grace," December 30, 2005, http://transcripts.cnn.com/TRANSCRIPTS/0512/30/ng.01.html.

[130] Dean Radin, *The Conscious Universe: The Scientific Truth of Psychic Phenomena* (New York: HarperCollins Publishers, 1997): 118-124.

[131] Radin, *The Conscious Universe*.

[132] Charles Honorton and Diane C. Ferrari, "'Future telling': A meta-analysis of forced-choice precognition experiments, 1935-1987," *Journal of Parapsychology* 53 (December 1989): 281-308, https://citeseerx.ist.psu.edu/viewdoc/download?doi=10.1.1.397.9652&rep=rep1&type=pdf.

[133] Dan Penman, "Have scientists really proved that man can see into the future?" NewsMonster, May 9, 2007.

[134] Radin, *The Conscious Universe*, 101.

[135] Jessica Utts, "An Assessment of the Evidence for Psychic Functioning," *Journal of Scientific Exploration* 10, no. 1 (1996): 3-30.

[136] Radin, *The Conscious Universe*, 104.

[137] Radin, *The Conscious Universe*, 105.

[138] R. Targ and H. Puthoff, "Information transmission under conditions of sensory shielding," *Nature* 251 (1974): 602-607.

[139] Rodrigo Cofré et al., "Whole-Brain Models to Explore Altered States of Consciousness from the Bottom Up," *Brain Science* 10, no. 9 (September 2020): 626.

[140] Xiao-Peng Qu et al., "Long-Term Cognitive Improvement after Functional Hemispherectomy," *World Neurosurgery* (March 2020): 135.

[141] John Lorber and D. Voth, ed., "Is your brain really necessary?" *Hydrocephalus im frühen kindesalter: Fortschritte der grundlagenforschung, diagnostik und therapie* (Stuttgart: Enke, 1983), 2–14.

[142] Michael Nahm et al., "Discrepancy between Cerebral Structure and Cognitive Functioning," *The Journal of Nervous and Mental Disease* 205, no. 2 (December 1917): 967-968.

[143] R. Craig Hogan, *Your Eternal Self: Science Discovers the Afterlife* (Normal, IL: Greater Reality Publications, 2020), 15.

[144] Kimberly Clark Sharp, *After the Light* (Lincoln, NE: Authors Choice Press, 2003), 7-15.

[145] Kenneth Ring and Madelaine Lawrence, "Further evidence for veridical perception during near-death experiences," *Journal of Near-Death Studies* 11, no. 4 (June 1993): 223-229.

[146] Hogan, *Your Eternal Self*.

[147] S. W. Twemlow, G. O. Gabbard, and F. C. Jones, "The out-of-body experience: a phenomenological typology based on questionnaire responses," *American Journal of Psychiatry* 139, no. 4 (April 1982): 450-5.

[148] Frederick William Henry Myers, *Human Personality and Its Survival of Bodily Death* (London: Longmans, 1903).

[149] Twemlow, "The out-of-body experience."

[150] D. Scott Rogo, "Researching the out-of-body experiences," cited in Schmicker, *Best Evidence*, 203.

151 "Physicists Challenge Notion of Electric Nerve Impulses; Say Sound More Likely," science blog, University of Copenhagen, March 7, 2007, https://scienceblog.com/12738/physicists-challenge-notion-of-electric-nerve-impulses-say-sound-more-likely/.

152 Jeffrey Long with Paul Perry, *The Science of Near-Death Experiences* (New York: HarperOne, 2010), 80.

153 Peter Fenwick, "Dying: a spiritual experience as shown by Near Death Experiences and Deathbed Visions," unpublished paper, 2004, https://www.rcpsych.ac.uk/docs/default-source/members/sigs/spirituality-spsig/spirituality-special-interest-group-publications-pfenwickneardeath.pdf?sfvrsn=686898bc_2.

154 Peter Fenwick & Elizabeth Fenwick, E., *The Truth in the Light—An Investigation of Over 300 Near-Death Experiences* (Headline Book Publishing, 1996).

155 Spink Health, "One in 10 people have 'near-death' experiences, according to new study," EurekAlert, June 28, 2019, https://www.eurekalert.org/pub_releases/2019-06/sh-oi1062519.php.

156 Sarah Tippit, "Scientist Says Mind Continues after Brain Dies," Reuters, June 29, 2001.

157 Tippit, "Scientist Says Mind Continues."

158 Michael Sabom, *Light and Death* (Grand Rapids, Michigan: Zondervan, 1998).

159 Edward Kelly et al., *Irreducible Mind: Toward a Psychology for the 21st Century* (Lanham, MD: Rowman & Littlefield Publishers, 2006).

160 Sabom, *Light and Death*.

161 Gary Habermas, "Near Death Experiences and the Evidence—A Review Essay," LBTS Faculty Publications and Presentations, fall 1996, 337.

162 Melvin Morse and Paul Perry, *Closer to the Light: Learning from the Near-Death Experiences of Children* (New York: Random House, 1990), 152-154.

163 Dossey, *Recovering the Soul*, 18.

164 Pim Van Lommel, "Near-death experience in survivors of cardiac arrest; a prospective study in the Netherlands," *Lancet* 358 (December 15, 2001): 2039-45.

165 Bruce Greyson, "Near death experiences as evidence for survival of bodily death," Esalen Center for Theory & Research Conference on Survival of Bodily Death, February 11-16, 2000.

166 Nancy L. Roberts, "Physician finds God in studies of near-death experiences," *The Compass*, February 3, 2017, https://www.thecompassnews.org/2017/02/physician-finds-god-studies-near-death-experiences/.

167 Farr Curlin et al., "Religious Characteristics of U.S. Physicians: A National Survey," *Journal of General Internal Medicine* 20, no. 7 (July 2005): 629-634.

168 Ronald Pearson, *Intelligence Behind the Universe!* (London: Headquarters Publishing Company, 1990).

169 Jan Vandersande, *Life After Death: Some of the Best Evidence* (Denver: Outskirts Press, 2008).

170 Tymn, "Distinguished researchers."

171 Tymn, "Distinguished researchers."

172 J. J. Snyder, "Science confirms survival," The Campaign for Philosophical Freedom, www.cfpf.org.uk/articles/background/snyder.html.

173 Tymn, "Distinguished researchers."

174 Tymn, "Distinguished researchers."

175 Tymn, "Distinguished researchers."

176 Tymn, "Distinguished researchers."

177 Tymn, "Distinguished researchers."

178 Tymn, "Distinguished researchers."

179 Tymn, "Distinguished researchers."

180 Tymn, "Distinguished researchers."

181 Tymn, "Distinguished researchers."

182 Tymn, "Distinguished researchers."

183 Tymn, "Distinguished researchers."

184 Tymn, "Distinguished researchers."

185 Tymn, "Distinguished researchers."

186 J. L. Baird, *Sermons, Soap and Television—Autobiographical Notes* (London: Royal Television Society, 1988).

Endnotes

[187] G. Meek, *After We Die, What Then?* (Columbus, OH: Ariel Press, 1987).

[188] Archie Roy, Letter to Michael Roll, May 19, 1983, *Campaign for Philosophical Freedom*, https://www.cfpf.org.uk/letters/1983/1983-05-19_ar2mr/1983-05-19_ar2mr.html.

[189] P. Bander, *Voices from the Tapes* (New York: Drake Publishers, 1973), 132.

[190] Bander, *Voices from the Tapes*.

[191] Elisabeth Lloyd Mayer, *Science, Skepticism, and the Inexplicable Powers of the Human Mind* (New York: Bantam Books, 2007).

[192] Tymn, "Distinguished researchers."

[193] Botkin, *Induced After-Death Communication*, 168.

[194] Cesare Lombroso, *Criminal Man* (Durham, NC: Duke University Press Books, 2006).

[195] Tymn, "Distinguished researchers."

[196] Greyson, "Near death experiences as evidence."

[197] Tymn, "Distinguished researchers."

[198] Tymn, "Distinguished researchers."

[199] Tymn, "Distinguished researchers."

[200] Tymn, "Distinguished researchers."

[201] Schwartz, *The Afterlife Experiments*.

[202] Tymn, "Distinguished researchers."

[203] Tymn, "Distinguished researchers."

[204] David Fontana, *Is There an Afterlife? A Comprehensive Overview of the Evidence* (Washington, D.C.: O Books, 2005).

[205] Tymn, "Distinguished researchers."

[206] Bander, *Voices from the Tapes*, 132.

[207] C. G. Jung, *Letters, Volume 1* (Princeton, NJ: Princeton University Press, 1973).

[208] Gustave Geley, *Clairvoyance and Materialization: A Record of Experiments* (London: T. Fisher Unwin Limited, 1927).

[209] Tymn, "Distinguished researchers."

[210] Tymn, "Distinguished researchers."

[211] Tymn, "Distinguished researchers."

[212] Tymn, "Distinguished researchers."

[213] Tymn, "Distinguished researchers."

[214] Tymn, "Distinguished researchers."

[215] Tymn, "Distinguished researchers."

[216] Michael Rogge, "Parapsychology and Personal Survival after Death," Man and the Unknown, 2019, https://wichm.home.xs4all.nl/paraps.html.

[217] H. Murphet, *Beyond death—The Undiscovered Country* (Wheaton, IL: Quest Books, 1990), 64.

[218] Arthur James Balfour, *A Defence of Philosophic Doubt; Being an Essay on the Foundations of Belief* (Sydney, Aus.: Wentworth Press, 2019).

[219] Tymn, "Distinguished researchers."

[220] V. Zammit, *A Lawyer Presents*.

[221] A. C. Doyle, *The History of Spiritualism, Vols. I and II* (New York: Arno Press, 1926).

[222] Zammit, *A Lawyer Presents*.

[223] Zammit, *A Lawyer Presents*.

[224] I. Funk, *The Psychic Riddle* (New York: Funk & Wagnalls Company, 1907).

[225] Tymn, "Distinguished researchers."

[226] Tymn, "Distinguished researchers."

[227] P. F. Brune, "The rediscovered beyond," World ITC, December 2006, www.worlditc.org/d_07_brune_rediscovered_beyond.htm.

[228] Bander, *Voices from the Tapes*.

[229] "The Church of England and Spiritualism—the full text of the Church of England committee appointed by Archbishop Lang and Archbishop Temple to investigate Spiritualism" (London: Psychic Press Ltd., 1939), https://www.cfpf.org.uk/articles/religion/cofe_report/cofe_report.html.

[230] John Hooper, "Dialogue with the Dead Is Feasible, Vatican Spokesman Says," *London Observer Service*, January 31, 1999.

[231] John Hooper, "Dialogue with the Dead Is Feasible, Vatican Spokesman Says," *London Observer Service*, January 31, 1999.

[232] Tymn, "Distinguished researchers."

[233] Tymn, "Distinguished researchers."

Bibliography

"Additional Annie Nanji Communications about Events in Dr. Nanji's Life." Afterlife Research and Education Institute, Inc. http://afterlifeinstitute.org/annie/.

Ananthaswamy, Anil. "What Does Quantum Theory Actually Tell Us about Reality?" *Scientific American blogs*. September 3, 2018. https://blogs.scientificamerican.com/observations/what-does-quantum-theory-actually-tell-us-about-reality/.

"Annie Describes a Business Meeting Over Lunch Dr. Nanji Had." Afterlife Research and Education Institute, Inc. http://afterlifeinstitute.org/lunch/.

"Annie Describes a Meeting Dr. Nanji Had with Jim and Elsie Ellis." Afterlife Research and Education Institute, Inc. http://afterlifeinstitute.org/blank/.

"Annie Gets Dr. Nanji's Thoughts as He Sees a Woman Who Looks Like Her." Afterlife Research and Education Institute, Inc. http://afterlifeinstitute.org/woman/.

"Annie Has Seen Their Gravestone." Afterlife Research and Education Institute, Inc. http://afterlifeinstitute.org/gravestone/.

"Annie Knows Dr. Nanji Was Annoyed That Seats in a Park Had Changed." Afterlife Research and Education Institute, Inc. http://afterlifeinstitute.org/park/.

"Annie Nanji Asks Dr. Nanji about a Ring and Lock of Hair." Afterlife Research and Education Institute, Inc. http://afterlifeinstitute.org/ring/.

"Annie Remarks that a Bedspread in the Flat Is Not Oriented Correctly." Afterlife Research and Education Institute, Inc. http://afterlifeinstitute.org/bedspread/.

"Annie Says She Went with Dr. Nanji to Visit a Friend, Gladys Hayter." Afterlife Research and Education Institute, Inc. www.afterlifeinstitute.org/gladys/.

Bibliography

"Annie Sees Dr. Nanji Going to the Cemetery Laying Flowers on Her Grave." Afterlife Research and Education Institute, Inc. http://afterlifeinstitute.org/cemetery/.

"Annie Talks about the Pictures in Dr. Nanji's Flat." Afterlife Research and Education Institute, Inc. http://afterlifeinstitute.org/pictures/.

"Antecedents & Discovery to 1867." Mysterious Planchette: A Survey of Curious Devices for Speaking to the Dead. www.mysteriousplanchette.com/History/history1.html.

Baird, J. L. *Sermons, Soap and Television—Autobiographical Notes.* London: Royal Television Society, 1988.

Balfour, Arthur James. *A Defence of Philosophic Doubt; Being an Essay on the Foundations of Belief.* Sydney, Aus.: Wentworth Press, 2019.

Balfour, Jean. "The 'Palm Sunday' Case: New Light on an Old Love Story." *Proceedings of the Society for Psychical Research* 52 (1960): 79-267.

Bander, P. *Voices from the Tapes.* New York: Drake Publishers, 1973.

Becker, Adam. *What Is Real?: The Unfinished Quest for the Meaning of Quantum Physics.* New York: Basic Books, 2018.

Beischel, Julie, and Gary Schwartz. "Anomalous information reception by research mediums demonstrated using a novel triple-blind protocol." *Explore* 3, no. 1 (January 2007).

Bennett, E. *Apparitions and Haunted Houses: A Survey of Evidence.* London: Faber and Faber, 1939.

Bissler, Jane. "Voices Across the Veil Direct Personal Communication." https://voicesacrosstheveil.afterlifedata.com/direct-personal-communication

Blum, Deborah. *Ghost Hunters: William James and the Search for Scientific Proof of Life After Death.* New York: Penguin Press, 2006.

Bibliography

Botkin, Allan L., and R. Craig Hogan. *Induced After-Death Communication: A Miraculous Therapy for Grief and Loss.* Charlottesville, VA: Hampton Roads Publishing, 2014.

Braude, Stephen. "The Mediumship of Carlos Mirabelli (1889-1951)." *Journal of Scientific Exploration* 31, no. 3 (September 2017): 435-456.

Brune, P. F. "The rediscovered beyond." World ITC. December 2006. www.worlditc.org/d_07_brune_rediscovered_beyond.htm.

Burt, Cyril. *The Gifted Child.* New York: Wiley, 1975.

Carter, Chris. "Rebuttal to Keith Augustine's attack of 'Does Consciousness Depend on the Brain?'" Accessed May 30, 2007. www.survivalafterdeath.info/articles/carter/augustine.htm.

Chalmers, David. "The Puzzle of Conscious Experience." *Scientific American* 26, no. 3 (summer 1917). Special issue "Mysteries of the mind."

"The Church of England and Spiritualism—the full text of the Church of England committee appointed by Archbishop Lang and Archbishop Temple to investigate Spiritualism." London: Psychic Press Ltd., 1939. https://www.cfpf.org.uk/articles/religion/cofe_report/cofe_report.html.

Clark Sharp, Kimberly. *After the Light.* Lincoln, NE: Authors Choice Press, 2003.

Cofré, Rodrigo, Rubén Herzog, Pedro A.M. Mediano, Juan Piccinini, Fernando E. Rosas, Yonatan Sanz Perl, and Enzo Tagliazucchi. "Whole-Brain Models to Explore Altered States of Consciousness from the Bottom Up." *Brain Science* 10, no. 9 (September 2020): 626.

"Completed Studies." Windbridge Research Center. https://www.windbridge.org/research/completed-studies/.

Crowley, Ronan, and Geert Lernout. "Joseph MacCabe in Ulysses." *Genetic Joyce Studies* 12 (Spring 2012).

Curlin, Farr, John Lantos, Chad Roach, Sarah Sellergren, and Marshall Chin. "Religious Characteristics of U.S. Physicians: A National Survey." *Journal of General Internal Medicine* 20, no. 7 (July 2005): 629-634.

"David Thompson ~ Materialization Medium." Afterlife Research and Education Institute, Inc. http://afterlifeinstitute.org/david/.

De Goes, Eurico. *Prodígios da Biopsychica obtidos com o Médium Mirabelli*. São Paulo: Typographia Cupol, 1937.

"Direct Voice: Conversation between mother and her deceased son." Man and the unknown. Michael Rogge. August 17, 1996. www.xs4all.nl/~wichm/fearon.html.

Dossey, Larry. *Recovering the Soul: A Scientific and Spiritual Search*. Bloomington, Indiana: iUniverse, 2008.

"Douglas and Eira Conacher Communicate after Douglas's Body Has Died." Afterlife Research and Education Institute, Inc. http://afterlifeinstitute.org/conachers/.

Doyle, A. C. *The History of Spiritualism, Vols. I and II*. New York: Arno Press, 1926.

"Dr. Nanji Says He Hears Her Taps in His Flat." Afterlife Research and Education Institute, Inc. http://afterlifeinstitute.org/tapping/.

Duncan, Helen, and C. E. Bechhofer Roberts. *The Trial of Mrs. Duncan*. London: Jarrolds Publishers, 1945.

"Examples from Sonia Rinaldi's Work Showing the People Are Alive." Afterlife Research and Education Institute, Inc. http://afterlifeinstitute.org/sonia/.

Fenwick, Peter. "Approaching-Death Experiences and the NDE: A Model for the Dying Process?" IANDS, June 24, 2017. https://www.iands.org/research/nde-research/important-research-articles/42-dr-peter-fenwick-md-science-and-spirituality.html?start=5.

Fenwick, Peter. "Dying: a spiritual experience as shown by Near Death Experiences and Deathbed Visions." Unpublished paper, 2004. https://www.rcpsych.ac.uk/docs/default-source/members/sigs/spirituality-spsig/spirituality-special-interest-group-publications-pfenwickneardeath.pdf?sfvrsn=686898bc_2.

Flint, Leslie, Douglas Conacher, and Eira Conacher. *Chapters of Experience.* London: Muller, 1973.

Fontana, David. *Is There an Afterlife? A Comprehensive Overview of the Evidence.* Washington, D.C.: O Books, 2005.

Funk, I. *The Psychic Riddle.* New York: Funk & Wagnalls Company, 1907.

Galvan, Jill. "Tennyson's Ghosts: The Psychical Research Case of the Cross-Correspondences, 1901-c.1936." Branch Collective. https://www.branchcollective.org/?ps_articles=jill-galvan-tennysons-ghosts-the-psychical-research-case-of-the-cross-correspondences-1901-c-1936.

Gauld, Alan. *Mediumship and Survival: A Century of Investigations.* London: Heinemann, 1982.

Geley, Gustave. *Clairvoyance and Materialization: A Record of Experiments.* London: T. Fisher Unwin Limited, 1927.

Greyson, Bruce. "Near death experiences as evidence for survival of bodily death." Esalen Center for Theory & Research Conference on Survival of Bodily Death. February 11-16, 2000.

Guggenheim, Bill, and Judy Guggenheim. *Hello from Heaven.* New York: Bantam, 1995.

Gurney, Edmund, Frank Podmore, and Frederic William Henry Myers. *Phantasms of the Living.* London: Trubner, 1886.

Habermas, Gary. "Near Death Experiences and the Evidence—A Review Essay." LBTS Faculty Publications and Presentations. Fall 1996.

Haisch, Bernard. "Quantum Mechanics and Consciousness: A New Measurement." Presentation, 27th Annual Society for Scientific Exploration Conference, Boulder, CO, 2008.

Hameroff, Stuart. "Overview: Could life and consciousness be related to the fundamental quantum nature of the universe?" *Quantum Consciousness*. www.quantumconsciousness.org/content/overview-sh.

Hamilton, Trevor. "The Cross-Correspondences." Psi Encyclopedia. March 24, 2017. https://psi-encyclopedia.spr.ac.uk/articles/cross-correspondences.

Hapgood, Charles H. *Voices of Spirit*. New York: Delacorte Press / Seymour Lawrence, 1975.

Haraldsson, Erlendur. "Survey of claimed encounters with the dead." *Omega* 19 (1989).

Hay, David. "The spirituality of the unchurched." *Mission and Spirituality* (2002).

"Helen Duncan's Trial Witnesses Testify People They Knew Materialized in Her Séances." Afterlife Research and Education Institute, Inc. http://afterlifeinstitute.org/witnesses/.

"Herbert Carmichael Irwin." This Day in Aviation. https://www.thisdayinaviation.com/tag/herbert-carmichael-irwin/.

Hodgson, Richard. "A further record of observations of certain phenomena of a trance." *Proceedings of the Society for Psychical Research* 13 (1897-1898).

Hogan, R. Craig. *There Is Nothing but Mind and Experiences*. Normal, IL: Greater Reality Publications, 2020.

Hogan, R. Craig. *Your Eternal Self: Science Discovers the Afterlife*. Normal, IL: Greater Reality Publications, 2020.

Holden, Jan. "J. Holden describes the frequency of after-death communication." University of North Texas News Service. November 5, 2005.

Holzer, Hans. *Ghost Hunter*. New York: Bobbs Merrill Company, 1963.

Honorton, Charles, and Diane C. Ferrari. "'Future telling': A meta-analysis of forced-choice precognition experiments, 1935-1987." *Journal of Parapsychology* 53 (December 1989): 281-308. https://citeseerx.ist.psu.edu/viewdoc/download?doi=10.1.1.397.9652&rep=rep1&type=pdf.

Hyslop, James H. *Life After Death: Problems of the Future Life and Its Nature*. Whitefish, MT: Kessinger Publishing, 1918.

Johnson, R. C. *The Imprisoned Splendour*. Wheaton, IL: Quest Books, 1982.

Jung, C. G. *Letters, Volume 1*. Princeton, NJ: Princeton University Press, 1973.

Kak, Subhash, Deepak Chopra, and Means Kafatos. "Perceived reality, quantum mechanics, and consciousness." *Cosmology* 18 (2014): 231-245.

Kalish, Richard A., and David K. Reynolds. "Phenomenological reality and post death contact." *Journal for the Scientific Study of Religion* (1973).

Kelly, Edward, Emily Kelly, Adam Crabtree, and Alan Gauld. *Irreducible Mind: Toward a Psychology for the 21st Century*. Lanham, MD: Rowman & Littlefield Publishers, 2006.

Komp, Diane. *A Window to Heaven: When Children See Life in Death*. Grand Rapids, Michigan: Zondervan Publishing, 1992.

"Konstantin Raudive Speaks from Spirit to Sonia Rinaldi." Afterlife Research and Education Institute, Inc. http://afterlifeinstitute.org/raudive/.

Kübler-Ross, Elisabeth. *On Children and Death*. New York: MacMillan Publishing, 1983.

Kübler-Ross, Elisabeth. *On Life after Death*. Berkeley, CA: Celestial Arts, 2008.

Lambright, Claudia Carlton. *Just a Dream Away: After-Death Communication through Dreams*. Self-published, December 7, 2020.

Leslie Flint Educational Trust, 22B Brunswick Park, London SE5 7RJ, England, www.leslieflint.com.

Lewin, R. "Is your brain really necessary?" *Science* 210, no. 4475 (December 12, 1980): 1232–1234.

"Life After Death: Episode 8, The testimony of science." Hosted by Tom Harpur. TV documentary. Directed by Dan Robinson. Aired 1996.

Lodge, Sir Oliver. *Raymond or Life and Death*. New York: George H. Doran, 1916.

Lombroso, Cesare. *Criminal Man*. Durham, NC: Duke University Press Books, 2006.

Long, Jeffrey, with Paul Perry. *The Science of Near-Death Experiences*. New York: HarperOne, 2010.

Lorber, John. D. Voth, ed. "Is your brain really necessary?" In Hydrocephalus im frühen kindesalter: Fortschritte der grundlagenforschung, diagnostik und therapie. Stuttgart: Enke, 1983.

Maddox, John. "The Unexpected Science to Come." *Scientific American* 281 (December 1999): 62-67.

Matchett, William. "Repeated hallucinatory experiences as part of the mourning process among Hopi Indian women." Psychiatry 35, no. 2 (May 1972).

Mayer, Elisabeth Lloyd. *Science, Skepticism, and the Inexplicable Powers of the Human Mind*. New York: Bantam Books, 2007.

McKenzie, A. *Apparitions and Ghosts: A Modern Study*. London: Arthur Baker Ltd., 1971.

"Medium Alice Holland, England. UK." Psychic Truth. http://psychictruth.info/Medium_Alice_Holland.htm.

Meek, G. *After We Die, What Then?* Columbus, OH: Ariel Press, 1987.

Meek, G., et al. *Spiricom: An Electronic-Etheric Systems Approach to Communications with Other Levels of Human Consciousness*. Metascience Research, 1982.

Michael Fearon – Speaking to Alice Fearon." Afterlife Research and Education Institute, Inc. http://afterlifeinstitute.org/fearon/.

"Mirabelli, Carlos Carmine." The Free Dictionary by Farlex. https://encyclopedia2.thefreedictionary.com/Mirabelli%2c+Carlos+Carmine.

"Montague Keen Speaks to Sitters Who Know Him in a Séance." Afterlife Research and Education Institute, Inc. http://afterlifeinstitute.org/monty/.

Moody, Raymond. "Dreams as Communication from the Afterlife." April 27, 2021. https://lifeafterlife.com/blog/dreams-as-communication-from-the-afterlife/.

Moody, Raymond. "Family Reunions: Visionary Encounters with the Departed in a Modern-Day Psychomanteum." *Journal of Near-Death Studies* 11, no. 2 (Winter 1992): 112.

Moore, C. A. "The unseen realm: Science is making room for near-death experiences beyond this world." *Desert Morning News*. February 18, 2006.

Morse, Melvin. "Near-death experiences and death-related visions in children: implications for the clinician." *Current Problems in Pediatrics* 24 (1994).

Morse, Melvin, and Paul Perry. *Closer to the Light: Learning from the Near-Death Experiences of Children.* New York: Random House, 1990.

Morse, Melvin, with Paul Perry. *Parting Visions.* New York: Villard Books, 1994.

Murphet, H. *Beyond death — The Undiscovered Country.* Wheaton, IL: Quest Books, 1990.

Myers, Frederick William Henry. *Human Personality and Its Survival of Bodily Death.* London: Longmans, 1903.

Nahm, Michael, David Rousseau, and Bruce Greyson. "Discrepancy between Cerebral Structure and Cognitive Functioning." *The Journal of Nervous and Mental Disease* 205, no. 2 (December 1917): 967-968.

Osis, Karlis, and Erlendur Haraldsson. *At the Hour of Death.* Norwalk, CT: Hastings House, 1997.

"Parent Responses to Sheri Perl Voice Recordings." Afterlife Research and Education Institute, Inc. http://afterlifeinstitute.org/perl/.

Parnia, Sam, Ken Spearpoint, Gabriele de Vos, Peter Fenwick, Diana Goldberg, Jie Yang, Jiawen Zhu, Katie Baker, Hayley Killingback, Paula McLean, Melanie Wood, A. Maziar Zafari, Neal Dickert, Roland Beisteiner, Fritz Sterz, Michael Berger, Celia Warlow, Siobhan Bullock, Salli Lovett, Russell Metcalfe Smith McPara, Sandra Marti-Navarette, Pam Cushing, Paul Wills, Kayla Harris, Jenny Sutton, Anthony Walmsley, Charles D. Deakin, Paul Little, Mark Farber, Bruce Greyson, and Elinor R Schoenfeld. "Aware—Awareness during Resuscitation—A prospective study." *Resuscitation* 85, no. 12 (December 1, 2014): 1799-1805.

Patt, Stephan. "Brain localization of consciousness? Neurological considerations." Lecture, 7th International Interdisciplinary Seminar, Exploring the Human Mind: The Perspective of Natural Sciences. Ponte di Legno, Italy. December 28, 2003.

Pearson, Ronald. *Intelligence Behind the Universe!* London: Headquarters Publishing Company, 1990.

Penman, Dan. "Have scientists really proved that man can see into the future?" NewsMonster. May 9, 2007.

Phillips, J. B. *Ring of Truth.* London: H. Shaw, 1977.

"Physical Mediumship Conversation: Sarah Communicates with Her Love in Spirit." Afterlife Research and Education Institute, Inc. http://afterlifeinstitute.org/sarah-nick/.

"Physicists Challenge Notion of Electric Nerve Impulses; Say Sound More Likely." Science blog. University of Copenhagen. March 7, 2007. https://scienceblog.com/12738/physicists-challenge-notion-of-electric-nerve-impulses-say-sound-more-likely/.

"Planchette Writing." The Daoist Encyclopedia: FYSK Daoist Culture Centre Database. https://en.daoinfo.org/wiki/Planchette_Writing.

Presti, David E. "Book Review: Irreducible Mind: Toward a Psychology for the 21st Century." *Journal of Near-Death Studies* (Autumn 2008): 64.

Price, Harry. *Leaves from a Psychist's Case-Book*. London: Victor Gollancz, 1933.

"Psychic Detectives." Transcript. CNN. "Nancy Grace." December 30, 2005. http://transcripts.cnn.com/TRANSCRIPTS/0512/30/ng.01.html.

Qu, Xiao-Peng, Yan Qu, Chao Wang, and Bei Liu. "Long-Term Cognitive Improvement after Functional Hemispherectomy." *World Neurosurgery* (March 2020): 135.

Radin, Dean. *The Conscious Universe: The Scientific Truth of Psychic Phenomena*. New York: HarperCollins Publishers, 1997.

Raudive, Konstantin. *Breakthrough: An Amazing Experiment in Electronic Communication with the Dead*, Colin Smythe Ltd, 1971.

"The Return of Montgague [sic] Keen." Victor Zammit. https://victorzammit.com/MontagueKeentapes/Montague%20Keen%20-%20transcript16thApril2004.htm.

Ring, Kenneth, and Sharon Cooper. *Mindsight: Near-Death and Out-of-Body Experiences in the Blind*. Bloomington, Indiana: iUniverse, 2008.

Ring, Kenneth, and Madelaine Lawrence. "Further evidence for veridical perception during near-death experiences." *Journal of Near-Death Studies* 11, no. 4 (June 1993): 223-229.

Roberts, Nancy L. "Physician finds God in studies of near-death experiences." *The Compass*. February 3, 2017. https://www.thecompassnews.org/2017/02/physician-finds-god-studies-near-death-experiences/.

Rogge, Michael. "Parapsychology and Personal Survival after Death." Man and the Unknown. 2019. https://wichm.home.xs4all.nl/paraps.html.

Rogo, D. Scott. *Leaving the Body: A Complete Guide to Astral Projection.* New York: Fireside/Simon & Schuster, 1993.

Rogo, D. Scott. "Researching the out-of-body experiences." Cited in Schmicker, *Best Evidence*, 203.

Rosenblum, Bruce, and Fred Kuttner. *The Quantum Enigma.* Oxford: Oxford University Press, 2011.

Roy, Archie. Letter to Michael Roll. May 19, 1983. *Campaign for Philosophical Freedom.* https://www.cfpf.org.uk/letters/1983/1983-05-19_ar2mr/1983-05-19_ar2mr.html.

Sabom, Michael. *Light and Death.* Grand Rapids, Michigan: Zondervan, 1998.

Schmicker, Michael. *Best Evidence.* Lincoln, NE: Writers Club Press, 2002.

Schwartz, Gary, Linda G. S. Russek, Lonnie A. Nelson, and Christopher Barentsen. "Accuracy and Replicability of Anomalous After-Death Communication Across Highly Skilled Mediums." *Journal of the Society for Psychical Research* 65 (2001): 1-25.

Schwartz, Gary, and W. L. Simon. *The Afterlife Experiments.* New York: Atria Books, 2003.

Smith, G. *The Unbelievable Truth.* Carlsbad, CA: Hay House, 2004.

Snyder, J. J. "Science confirms survival." The Campaign for Philosophical Freedom. www.cfpf.org.uk/articles/background/snyder.html.

Spink Health. "One in 10 people have 'near-death' experiences, according to new study." EurekAlert. June 28, 2019. https://www.eurekalert.org/pub_releases/2019-06/sh-oi1062519.php.

Spraggett, A. *The Case for Immortality.* Scarborough, Canada: New American Library of Canada, 1974.

Stevenson, Ian. "Do we need a new word to supplement 'hallucination'?" *American Journal of Psychiatry* 140 (1983).

Targ, R., and H. Puthoff. "Information transmission under conditions of sensory shielding." *Nature* 251 (1974): 602-607.

"A Theology of Ghosts." Thoughts of Loy. Loy Mershimer blogspot. September 19, 2005. http://loymershimer.blogspot.com/2005/09/theology-of-ghosts.html.

Tippit, Sarah. "Scientist Says Mind Continues after Brain Dies." Reuters. June 29, 2001.

Touber, Tijn. "Life goes on." *Ode* 3, no. 10 (December 2005).

Truscott, Andrew. "Experiment Confirms Quantum Theory Weirdness." Press release. Australian National University. ScienceDaily. May 27, 2015. https://www.sciencedaily.com/releases/2015/05/150527103110.htm.

Twemlow, S. W., G. O. Gabbard, and F. C. Jones. "The out-of-body experience: a phenomenological typology based on questionnaire responses." *American Journal of Psychiatry* 139, no. 4 (April 1982): 450-5.

Tymn, Michael. "Distinguished researchers found evidence for survival." After-Death Communication. https://kuriakon00.tripod.com/after_death_communication/research.html.

Tymn, Michael. "A veridical death-bed vision." Paranormal and Life After Death. March 14, 2008. https://paranormalandlifeafterdeath.blogspot.com/2008/03/.

Utts, Jessica. "An Assessment of the Evidence for Psychic Functioning." In "An Evaluation of Remote Viewing: Research and Applications." Michael Mumford, Andrew Rose, and David Goslin, eds. Washington, DC: American Institutes for Research. September 29, 1995.

"Validity of the Leslie Flint Afterlife Recordings." Afterlife Research and Education Institute, Inc. http://afterlifeinstitute.org/validity/.

Van Lommel, Pim. "Near-death experience in survivors of cardiac arrest; a prospective study in the Netherlands." *Lancet* 358 (December 15, 2001).

Vandersande, Jan. *Life After Death: Some of the Best Evidence.* Denver: Outskirts Press, 2008.

Vargas, Lawrence, F. Loya, and J. Hodde-Vargas. "Exploring the multidimensional aspects of grief reactions." *American Journal of Psychiatry* 146, no. 11 (1989).

Wagner, Stephen. "Deathbed visions." Liveabout.com. January 2, 2019. http://paranormal.about.com/library/weekly/aa021901a.htm.

Walia, Arjun. "'Consciousness Creates Reality'—Physicists Admit the Universe Is Immaterial, Mental, & Spiritual." Transcend Media Service. April 20, 2015. Citing R. C. Henry, "The Mental Universe," Nature 436, 2005: 29, quoting Sir James Jeans. https://www.transcend.org/tms/2015/04/consciousness-creates-reality-physicists-admit-the-universe-is-immaterial-mental-spiritual/.

"Why Pioneer Neurosurgeon Wilder Penfield Said the Mind Is More than the Brain." Interview of Michael Egnor by Robert J. Marks. Mind Matters News. Podcast audio. February 29, 2020. https://mindmatters.ai/2020/02/why-pioneer-neurosurgeon-wilder-penfield-said-the-mind-is-more-than-the-brain/.

Williams, Kevin. "Edgar Cayce on Dreams." June 28, 2020. online post, https://near-death.com/edgar-cayce-on-dreams/.

Wills-Brandon, Carla. *One Last Hug Before I Go: The Mystery and Meaning of Deathbed Visions.* Norwalk, CT: Hastings House, 2007.

Wilson, Colin. *Afterlife: An Investigation.* New York: Doubleday, 1987.

Woolworth, Tim. "Konstantin Raudive and His ITC EVP Breakthrough." ITC Voices. February 6, 2011. http://itcvoices.org/konstantin-raudive-and-his-itc-evp-breakthrough/.

Wright, Rochelle, and R. Craig Hogan. Repair & Reattachment Grief Therapy. Chicago: Greater Reality Publications, 2015.

Zammit, Victor. "Australian psychics beat 'orthodox' science." Victor Zammit. Accessed May 13, 2007. http://victorzammit.com/articles/sensingmurder.html.

Zammit, Victor. *A Lawyer Presents the Case for the Afterlife.* Sydney, Australia: Ganmell Pty. Ltd., 2006.